EVERY MILE A MEMORY

Partha Sarthi Sen Sharma is a graduate from Delhi University and is currently living in Lucknow, India. He is an Indian Administrative Service Officer and has written articles, mainly travel pieces, for *The Times of India*, *The Hindustan Times*, *Discover India*, *Swagat*, *Rail Bandhu* and other periodicals. He also published a travelogue titled *A Passage Across Europe* in 2011 and *Love Side by Side,* his fiction novel, in 2015. Apart from his work and writing, Partha loves to spend time with his family. He is an avid traveller, having travelled to over twenty countries. He is a voracious reader, who can read in English, Hindi and Bangla and is a sport enthusiast.

EVERY
MILE
A
MEMORY

PARTHA SARTHI SEN SHARMA

RUPA

Published by
Rupa Publications India Pvt. Ltd 2016
7/16, Ansari Road, Daryaganj
New Delhi 110002

Sales centres:
Allahabad Bengaluru Chennai
Hyderabad Jaipur Kathmandu
Kolkata Mumbai

ISBN: 978-81-291-4230-6

First impression 2016
10 9 8 7 6 5 4 3 2 1

The moral right of the author has been asserted.

Typeset by Saanvi Graphics, Noida.

Printed at HT Media Ltd., Noida

He who becomes the slave of habit,
who follows the same routes every day,
who never changes pace,
who does not risk and change the colour of his clothes,
who does not speak and does not experience,
dies slowly.

— Pablo Neruda

Contents

PART 2
CRISSCROSSING THE CONTINENT

An Introduction

Regardless of the various virtues of travel that we may extol, the fact is that only a fortunate few of us have the time, money and opportunity to travel extensively. Only when the dire necessities of life and livelihood are taken care of does the idea of travel for pleasure or for adventure arise, and although, with increasing prosperity, an increasing number of Indians travel domestically and internationally for business and for pleasure, some exceptionally fortuitous circumstances led me to extensive travels more than once.

In the year 2013-2014, I took a break from my twenty-year-old career as a civil servant to accompany my wife, a fellow officer, as she went to live in London to pursue a higher education programme. Just six years ago, my own training had led me to travel throughout Europe; this time too, the weekends and breaks during her course gave us the opportunity to travel. So, accompanied by our teenage daughter, we travelled all over Britain during the weekends and to continental Europe, Morocco and Turkey during the longer vacations. Later, on our return to India, despite a hectic work schedule, my natural penchant for travel and my curious mind that tries to make the most of even short-day trips to relatively unremarkable places led me to continue travelling and to write about it.

However, although these travels act as the background to and a sort of platform for my writings, I like to believe that my writings are not merely a banal chronicling of my actions and activities but are more about the thoughts and feelings, memories and imaginations that those places and experiences invoked in my mind. Thousands of people have travelled to these places—London, Lake District, Scotland, Paris, Lucknow and Nainital—and will continue to do so, but the impressions they form and the images that are invoked are unique to each traveller. The unique place that Mussoorie holds in my mind is not the same as the place it holds for Ruskin Bond or Frank Alter, and the images that Kolkata, the 'City of Joy', forms in the mind of Dominique Lapierre or Paul Theroux, are not the images it forms in Satyajit Ray's mind. In a sense, no place is an absolute reality but only a series of reflected images in the minds of its residents, visitors, travellers and tourists. And so the following pages deal with those unique images that were formed when I, a middle-class, wholly urban, partially educated Indian, who grew up in the eighties and nineties of the last century, travelled through these places.

The book is divided into four unequal parts. The first part, 'A Bengali in Britain', deals with, as the name suggests, my stay in and my travels around various places in the island—from touristy places like Scotland and Cornwall to small villages and ordinary nooks and corners in the city of London. The second part, 'Criss-crossing the Continent', deals with my travels across the English Channel and through continental

Europe and my occasional travails during the journey. Unlike six years ago when I lived in continental Europe and, therefore, travelled far more, my travels this time were short and sweet. On the one hand I revisited Paris and Rome; on the other I was lucky to visit cities like Lyon and Florence, Zermatt and Barcelona that were completely new to me. But even as, on the surface, nothing much had changed, perhaps I myself had changed in the intervening through years and, Paris and Rome—their palaces, parks and rivers, light and air—all looked familiar, they were yet not exactly the same.

The third part of the book, 'Across the Straits', concerns itself with my travels in Turkey across the strait of Bosphorus and in Morocco across the Strait of Gibraltar. I had longed to travel in these two countries for long, and they had an inexplicable hold over my mind. To sip a cup of Turkish coffee while cruising across the Bosphorus, with the silhouette of the domes and minarets of the famous mosques of Istanbul as the backdrop, had been a lifelong dream, especially after I came across Orhan Pamuk's works. On the other hand, Morocco, with its tall Berbers, the rain swept aerodrome of Casablanca and the snow-capped Atlas Mountains merging with the dunes of Sahara, was even more exotic and other-worldly. And so this part of my travels was completely new and unfamiliar, as were my thoughts and feelings.

The fourth and last part of the book, 'An Indian in India', deals with my travels in India to touristy places like Nainital and also to places far off the beaten track. Some of these writings are about Lucknow, the city that I live in, and they show that travelling physically is not really required to do travel writing, as one's mind can travel over centuries and miles while one sits in a street corner café on a lazy Sunday afternoon. Some of these writings, not too many, have appeared in print before, in magazines and newspapers, and were apparently liked by many, as was my novel *Love Side by Side.* This gave me the courage to continue writing and complete this book despite an increasingly busy and hectic job assignment.

I don't know whether and how you, my dear reader, will react to the following pages. Will some of my thoughts find resonance with you and strike a familiar chord, will they make you wonder and cause you to think differently about these places? People perceive not just places differently, but also writings. I believe each of you will react to the following pages in your own unique way, guided by your own mind, culture, frame of reference, feelings and genes. So for every one of you, this book will hopefully end up being a bit different. I am looking forward to that, and to hearing from you, my dear reader—about what my words ended up as in your mind.

PART 1
A Bengali in Britain

London Diaries: Bloomsbury

For a very long time, the word 'Bloomsbury' for me was synonymous with the famous publishing house, and it was barely a couple of years ago that I learnt that Bloomsbury was the name of an area in central London, from where the publishing house must have got its name. However, at that time I had no idea that I would be living in Bloomsbury in the near future.

Etymologically, Bloomsbury owes its origin to the 'bury' or fortified manor of one Mr Blemond, who built the Bury on a rural patch outside London city. That rural patch is now Bloomsbury. However, apart from the name, Mr Blemond's contribution to present-day Bloomsbury is hard to detect. Today's Bloomsbury, with its numerous leafy and well laid out rectangular gardens or 'squares' as they are called, and bordered with buildings boasting bare brick façades, owes much to the Dukes of Bedford. One of the leading families in Britain, they substantially carved out the present geography and topography of Bloomsbury; and therefore one finds a Bedford plethora—Bedford square, Bedford place, Bedford street etc.—throughout Bloomsbury. There is also a life-size, stone statue of one of the Dukes, Francis, at the southern end of Russell Square—one of the more prominent squares in Bloomsbury—prominent enough to lend its name to the nearby metro station.

The garden or square that was nearest to where we stayed was Gordon Square, a beautifully maintained leafy rectangle with bridle paths criss-crossing through it. Gordon Square is bordered by iron grills, and it was a revelation and a complete surprise to find the bust of our own Rabindranath Tagore prominently situated at its very heart, at the very heart of London. Below the bust were engravings excerpted from the great poet's works—one in Bengali and the other its English translation. The bust was unveiled just two years ago by the Prince of Wales through the contribution of Tagore Centre, UK, about the existence of which, too, I had no prior knowledge of. Maybe because it was so unexpected—I suddenly felt proud as an Indian—and dare I say, as a Bengali— to find the respect that our own bard still enjoyed in the land of the Englishmen, whose knighthood he had rejected as a mark of protest against the brutal atrocities of Jallianwala Bagh. But of course, Tagore, despite his undoubted genius, might not have got the Nobel Prize had some of his British admirers and friends, most notably the celebrated poet W.B. Yeats, not introduced his talents to the larger world. Below the bust it was proudly proclaimed—'the first Asian Nobel laureate'. I also could not help nothing the irony that India, his home country, had failed to mark the centenary of his being awarded the Nobel Prize—he got the Nobel Prize in 1913. In a way it is quite fitting that the bust of the poet today stands in Bloomsbury, an area regarded as the academic and literary heart of London.

Tagore, as far as I know, never lived in Bloomsbury, although he visited London many times and even lived in London in his youth over an extended period of time. But another great man, as great in his own field as Tagore, John Maynard Keynes lived in Gordon Square for thirty years. There is a blue plaque put up on the façade of 46 Gordon Square—a simple, apparently Georgian building, one of the many bordering the park—by English Heritage commemorating Keynes's stay. Even though I was not a student of economics, Keynes and Keynesian economics have remained so much a matter of heated couldn't debate that even a layman like me help noticing Keynes's unique contribution to what we now call macroeconomic. Despite the heated denouncements of his theories and his prescriptions by modern-day neo-liberal economists, democratic, popular governments the world over worship Keynes, especially during times of recession.

Opposite Gordon Square stands quite an impressive church called Christ the King. Owing to its revived Gothic architectural style, the church, made of faded yellow Bath stone, appears almost medieval. But I learnt upon entering it that it was constructed in the mid-nineteenth century; going by the antiquity of churches in central London, that is quite recent. The church belonged to the Catholic Apostolic Creed—a small and oft-forgotten creed that originated in the mid-nineteenth century in Britain and has lost most of its appeal today. Much of the church was closed except a small but beautiful chapel that had been 'lent' to the Church of England. That afternoon, when I entered the chapel, it was very quiet and serene, and apart from two Chinese students, meditating or praying silently with their eyes closed, there was nobody else. The chapel was not grandiose like that of, say, St Paul's cathedral but on that afternoon, the rays of the sun entering through the huge stained-glass windows and falling on the altar gave the chapel surreal quality a rare. I sat there silently, trying to picturize the now closed church in its heyday: Victorian gentlemen in their dark suits and grey whiskers, and ladies in their elaborate gowns, all listening to the sermon from the pulpit. The image of Christ painted on the stained glass window directly above the altar and depicted as a king with a crown on his head must have looked down over devotees then in the same way it did now.

As I came out of the church into twenty-first century London and retraced my steps to my residence, the sunshine fell on my shoulders, to paraphrase John Denver's famous song. I realized what a huge difference sun makes to a Londoner's life. When I had entered the church barely half an hour ago, it had been gloomy and threateningly cloudy, but now the sky was a brilliant blue, and the distant white clouds appeared as beautiful and friendly as in an English painting. So with a song on my lips and sunshine on my shoulders I wandered away to return someday.

Diwali at Trafalgar Square

When one is abroad, one tends to miss the familiarity of India and everything it denotes on festivals like Durga Pooja and Diwali. Although we had been in London for barely a month and a half, I would be surprised if it was not the same even for Indians who had been living abroad for decades—not, though, for young people of Indian origin and brought up in Britain, whose parents or even grandparents migrated to this country. And so on one Sunday, a week before Diwali, I, out of curiosity googled 'Diwali London'. I was lucky that I did, since a grand, organized celebration of Diwali in London was to take place on that very day and, of all places, at Trafalgar Square—which to my mind is the very heart of London. The fact that Indians in London today manage to organize the Diwali festivities at Trafalgar Square, and that the mayor of London comes to take part, is a stark reflection of both the importance of Indians in London and of their acceptance by the British.

Almost a decade ago, a group of enthusiastic Indians conceived this idea, and since then every year Diwali festivities are organized at Trafalgar Square, with the active participation of a number of notable organizations like the Art of Living Foundation, the Brahmakumaris, the Swaminarayan group of Akshardham Temple fame, ISKCON and others. Although Diwali celebrations are also conducted by most of these organizations at their own premises in and around London—Trafalgar Square being Trafalgar Square—this celebration has become special.

And so, on the Sunday afternoon preceding Diwali, we were at Trafalgar Square, duly and dutifully, despite warnings of an impending storm issued by the weather office and amplified by the media. But we were not alone, hordes of Indians, from all parts of London and beyond, had gathered at Trafalgar Square, which, quite crowded normally because of tourists, was on that day filled to the brim. It was a large Diwali Mela with a huge idol of Lord Ganesha displayed prominently, the likes of which I had not seen anywhere on the occasion of Diwali in India. There were food stalls selling Indian foods along with world cuisines, and families could be seen gorging on the food. A huge stage covered in blue waterproof material, because of the danger of rain (ever imminent in London), saw famous artists like Bali Brahmbhatt and Anoushka Shankar, daughter of the late Pandit Ravi Shankar and now famous in her own right, performing to packed audiences. A host of not-so-famous but very talented young local artists were also given an opportunity to showcase their talents to a packed audience and TV crews. What an opportunity they had got—at Trafalgar Square, in the heart of London, below Nelson's Column, with the imposing façade and dome of the National Picture Gallery as backdrop.

To me, the most amazing part of these Diwali celebrations was seeing the British and people of different nationalities, many of them wearing traditional Indian dresses, enjoying themselves along with their Indian friends. The cosmopolitanism of London and the acceptance of the contribution of the Indian community in the life and prosperity of today's London were on display. I wonder how amazed General Henry Havelock, whose imposing statue stands in one corner of Trafalgar Square and whose tomb is situated in our hometown of Lucknow, would have been to witness these Diwali celebrations in London—a far cry from his days in 1857! I was suddenly reminded of the Lucknow Mahotsav, which would be underway shortly in Lucknow. At that moment all the distance melted away in my mind, the world seemed to be one, and I was not lonely anymore.

Across the Prime Meridian
at Greenwich

In our NCERT[1] geography textbooks in school, we had read about the zero degree longitude, the prime meridian, passing through a village called Greenwich, situated somewhere in the outskirts of London, and also about the Greenwich Mean Time (GMT), in respect to which the time zones of various countries were set. In many ways, both these concepts (the prime meridian and GMT), which gained currency due to the pioneering work done by astronomers and scientists at the former Royal Observatory, were symbolic of Britain's then dominant role in the world. Those days are long gone, but a visit to Greenwich, long since engulfed in the continuous expansion of London, is a worthwhile daytrip. It is a UNESCO Word Heritage Site and the courtyard of the museum (the erstwhile Royal Observatory), marks the point through which the prime

---

[1] National Council of Educational Research and Training

meridian passes. This is indicated by a metal strip for the benefit of the thousands of tourists who pour in every day.

Although many would prefer to travel to Greenwich aboard a boat on the Thames, we took a ride on another of London's icons—a red double-decker bus. If one has ample time, travelling in a window seat on the upper deck of a double-decker on a clear sunny day through the streets of central London is an excellent way to observe the city and its citizens. And so Bus No. 188 took us one fine Saturday to Greenwich, and we alighted in front of the famous clipper ship, *Cutty Sark*, which used to be the fastest ship in the world in her prime in the 1870s and, today, is permanently docked on the Thames at Greenwich, as a grand reminder of the days when it used to rule the waves.

Though Greenwich itself is not situated near the sea, a lot of its history and fame is associated with the maritime history of Britain. The presence of the *Cutty Sark* is only one reminder of the same. Another much grander reminder is the huge and impressive, twin domed structure that faces the Thames river-front. Today it is mainly a museum, but once was the Royal Naval College, and before that a hospital for injured sailors. Like many medieval buildings of London that were built after the Great Fire of 1666, the Old Royal Naval College (as it is now named) owes its inspiration to the great architect Sir Christopher Wren, who would have gained a place in history as Britain's greatest architect even had he designed nothing after St Paul's Cathedral.

Under each dome of the College stand impressive halls. One housed a beautiful chapel, where I could see, among other things, a tablet dedicated to the memory of graduates who lost their lives in different parts of India in

1857. The other building, the so-called Painted Hall, is really dazzling. Beautifully detailed and colourfully magnificent paintings cover every inch of its walls and ceiling, clearly an inspiration from the Sistine Chapel in Rome. However, the painter, Thornhill, not only painted gods and goddesses and mythological scenes in his larger, than, life paintings, as was usually done, but also clearly identifiable portraits of his patrons, of members of the royal household and even of himself. It was here that the body of Admiral Nelson was first brought back from the fatal but victorious Battle of Trafalgar, before being given its final resting place in St Paul's.

Unlike its owner, the blood-stained and historical jacket of Nelson remains in Greenwich, housed in the nearby National Maritime Museum among many other curiosities, interesting and educative objects that will interest not only scholars of naval history but also common citizens and tourists.

Just across is a reminder of Greenwich's historical association with the royal family. Henry VIII (the famous and infamous) and Queen Elizabeth I were both born here in a palace now long gone. In its place stands a building called the Queen's House. Built more than three hundred years ago, it has a rather *un*-palace like appearance. There are no great embellishments on its façade nor any majestic domes or towers, but it commands a clear view of the riverfront, between the twin domes of the College.

Greenwich is a place of many histories. It has a history of maritime warfare; it has a history steeped in the painstaking astronomical calculations of medieval scientists; and it has a history associated with royalty, which gives it the status of a Royal Borough of London. But if one has the ears one can also hear, through the centuries past, the footsteps of the common man in its markets. A history that is not recorded in museums or books, but the echoes of which still travel across time to startle an unsuspecting ear around some street corner, some afternoon.

As the evening fell and we started on our return journey, I felt that a day was not enough to do justice to Greenwich. Perhaps the best stories are those that do not tell all and that keep some things hidden in their hearts for the next time.

Remembering Nelson Mandela
in London

When we grew up in the eighties, Nelson Mandela was still in his prison cell, serving a twenty-seven year prison term for opposing, sometimes by violent means, the apartheid regime of South Africa. We knew about the existence of the apartheid regime very well since any cricketer who played in South Africa, as the West Indian fast bowler Colin Croft did, was banned from international cricket, and since none of those cricketers were ever Indian, a fact about which we can be justifiably proud, it didn't bother us too much. The first time, as I recall, I learnt about Mandela was through a poignant movie about his life on Doordarshan. Much later, in my youth, when Mandela was already the first black president of now democratic and post-apartheid South Africa, I read his long autobiography *The Long Walk to Freedom*.

Now, I found myself in London when the news of Mandela's death reached us. It was a remarkable coincidence that, at very moment, a new film based on his life, '*Mandela:*

Long Walk to Freedom', was premiering in London, in the presence of the Duke and Duchess of Cambridge. The next morning I found the newspapers full of platitudes and tributes by many important men and women in London, many of which seemed pre-written. But as I walked to Trafalgar square and saw a lone, old black woman standing, I wondered what she would make of this outpouring of sympathy and praise the Western world was showering on Mandela. Could she forget that it was here, in Trafalgar Square, that demonstrations were held by common Londoners demanding Mandela's release, when Her Majesty's government then incidentally lead by the same ruling party as now consistently refused to impose sanctions on the apartheid regime of South Africa and its leader rebuked the protestors by calling Mandela a terrorist. Could she forget that the same countries—today intervening in the affairs of oil-rich countries of the Middle East in the name of democracy and humanity—kept more than silent during those twenty-seven years, as the brutal regime of South Africa gloated over its success at the cost of the basic human rights of black people?

I walked towards the nearby Parliament Square where a now-famous statue of Mandela stood, the only statue of a non-white person in the square, at a lower height than others; whereas the statues of some famous British statesmen overlook the Parliament building of the world's oldest democracy. A small black girl stood in front of Mandela's statue paying her silent tribute to her hero, who was and is a hero to her parents and to her grandparents too. I guessed that she would not know, from the frenzy of media tributes that day when all the high and mighty of the world were congregating in South Africa to shower their tributes, that maybe her hero's years in prison and his countrymen's years of oppression could have been reduced if this Parliament had been more true to its avowed ideals then.

Everybody knows about the statue of Mandela that stands in Parliament Square today, but if one cross over the Thames, then just next to the Southbank Centre, one will find another life-sized bronze bust of Nelson Mandela, an older one but relatively unknown and therefore uncrowded. As I paid my silent tribute to this truly great man, I could not help but wonder whether this adulation of today would have been muted had he not decided, like a saint, to start South Africa's new regime under his stewardship with a remarkable spirit of reconciliation towards his erstwhile oppressors and had he not stood as a bulwark against the possibility of violence and retaliation by his black supporters or had he converted South Africa into a communist state.

Nelson Mandela was truly a great man, a saint in flesh, by his qualities, by his achievements, and more importantly by what he stood for—a world where no man would be able to oppress another. But one couldn't help wonder whether all the praise helped on him today were as saintly.

Incidentally, the other non-British statesman to be honoured with a statue in Parliament Square is Abraham Lincoln.

The Lord Mayor's Show

It was terrible weather that day, as was so often the case in London: a chilly, cloudy morning, with heavy rain and cold piercing one's bones. But regardless of the weather, we decided to venture out to witness the Lord Mayor's Show, since it took place only once a year, on the second Saturday of November, when the newly elected Lord Mayor of the City of London would move in a huge procession through the streets of London to swear his or her loyalty to the crown. This ritual, now mainly ceremonial, had been going on for the last almost eight hundred years since its inception in AD 1215 and had continued uninterrupted even during the terrible war years. It must have been difficult in 1940, with the Battle of Britain being fought over London's skies as the Royal Air Force (RAF) defended the city against the Luftwaffe's London Blitz. German bombs fell all over London every day and every night for months. It was testimony to both British love for traditions as well as British endurance that the Lord Mayor's Show had carried on despite all obstacles.

So we decided to leave the warm comfort of our rooms, and armed with umbrellas, and braving the rain, we walked south to Fleet Street to witness the procession. Fleet Street was once the headquarters of the most important newspapers of the English-speaking world, but today only the engravings in centuries-old walls of the offices of long-forgotten journals remain. It was difficult to imagine that, not so long ago, there used to be a River 'Fleet' that traversed central London, where Fleet Street stands today and from which it gets its name. We were standing in a crowd of people of all ages and from all walks of life: whole families covered in transparent raincoats, old British women with poppy flowers on their lapels, young college students with Starbucks mugs in their hands; some braving the rain in their clearly inadequate umbrellas, others taking shelter in the nearby church of St Dunstan, waiting for the procession to arrive.

Presently, the sound of heavy drumbeats reached us, and the first regiment of soldiers, with their heavy grey overcoats and tall black caps, could be seen in the distance. They were followed by two tall wicker giants—Gog and Magog—waving to the children. The story, or rather the stories, of Gog and Magog, the two giants, are intertwined with the mythology behind the origin of Britain itself, and the giants have adorned the Lord Mayor's procession for centuries.

Gog and Magog were followed by a procession of three cavalry regiments atop shining black stallions trotting majestically; then followed a glimpse of armour and artillery, a host of 'shows' by voluntary and charity organizations and 'liveried companies' (as trade associations are called here), bands of school and college students dancing and waving flags, processions of profit-making companies using this occasion for publicity, cadet corps, impressive horse-drawn carriages carrying dignitaries wearing medieval costumes and even some shows by foreign governments trying to promote tourism in their countries. I remember distinctly the samba dance of some tired-and aged-looking dancers, trying to promote tourism in Bolivia.

Despite the rain and the bad weather, the enthusiasm both among the performers and spectators was contagious. Naturally, it reminded me of my experiences of the Republic Day Parade in India, both in New Delhi where I grew up and in Lucknow. However, there was nobody taking the salute, and I missed the voice of Jasdev Singh of Doordarshan (a voice that would be eternally linked to memories of 26 January in an entire generation of Indians who grew up in the eighties and had a TV at home).

As is so often with things British, what appears to be is seldom what it actually is. So the Lord Mayor was not the mayor of London and that poor gentleman or woman, who was the elected and political 'real' mayor of the greater metropolitan area of London, was quite a different person and had no procession going for him or her. The 'Lord Mayor' is a largely ceremonial head of the 'City of London'—mark the capital C—a historic a borough among the thirty-odd boroughs that make up London today. In the hoary past, the Lord Mayor, although never elected directly by the citizens even to this day, was the representative of the civil population, the aam admi, so to say.

The relationship of the citizens of London, especially of the trading and merchant classes, to the Monarch of England and the Monarch's authority over them had always a special and unique quality about it; and therefore it was decided that the city and its citizens would get some unique privileges, but at the same time the Crown's authority needed to be re-emphasized every year, whereby the newly elected Lord Mayor would move with his entire entourage to pay obeisance to the Monarch.

Of course it has now been centuries since the authority of the Crown has become titular—and that of the Lord Mayor too—but the tradition of the Lord Mayor's Show, that once used to take place on the River Thames with ceremonially and gaily decorated boats, continues to this day.

The procession we were watching was drawing to a close, with the arrival of the Lord Mayor in her carriage. She was a successful lawyer called Fiona Woolf, only the second woman in almost eight hundred years to grace this post. She waved good-naturedly at the assembled crowd, as her carriage, all gold and glitter, exquisitely and ostentatiously carved and polished, pulled by beautiful black stallions of abundant mane, moved along the street towards the Royal Courts of Justice, where she was to pledge her symbolic allegiance to the Crown in the presence of the judges of the High Court and then to return later with her procession. The more-than-two- centuries-old carriage was an impressive piece of both art and history and resided normally at the London Transport Museum in West End, from where it was borrowed every year for the procession, which was its original purpose.

In the evening, we, along with scores of Londoners assembled along the embankments of the river Thames, witnessed the majestic fireworks that marked the end of the Lord Mayor's Show every year, on the south bank of the Thames, between the Waterloo Bridge and Blackfriars's Bridge. The whole sky was lit up over the river in gold, blue, green and red, and for a brief fifteen minutes, the exquisite Mehtaabs dazzled the London sky, against the backdrop of the dome of St Paul's and the London Eye. This somewhat made up for me—the Diwali that had recently gone by. As we walked back to our residence that Saturday night, I felt that I had been lucky to witness an annual feature of London that was so much a part of its history and culture, and that gave a fleeting glimpse of London's heart beating through the centuries past.

Following the Steps of an Indian Revolutionary

We resided in the University area of London, very near the Senate House of the University. Nearby stands the University College of London. Every day I saw scores of students from the Indian subcontinent, as you wouldn't really distinguish between an Indian, a Pakistani or a Bangladeshi, rushing to attend their classes or simply relaxing in company of friends. But I imagined it had not always been so; a hundred or so years ago, Indian students, far fewer in number then, would have felt the distance and isolation—both geographically and culturally, would have experienced racism and discrimination, as well as a sense of shame in belonging to a conquered nation. While most learnt to live with such discomforts and went on with their studies becoming lawyers and ICS officers, for some it was a bit too much to bear.

Here, in University College of London, in its department of mechanical engineering, studied a young Indian man. He lodged with an English landlady at Ladbury Road, near Baker Street, the famous address of the fictional character Sherlock

Holmes created hardly a decade earlier. But he used to visit a hostel for Indian students at Highgate, opened by Shyamji Krishna Verma, an almost forgotten Indian revolutionary and a man of some means. Maybe under the influence of some of the other young Indian revolutionary students there (one of them was Veer Savarkar), this young man decided to commit an act of revolutionary violence to highlight the plight of an oppressed nation, to expose the hypocrisy of the then British government, which espoused all noble aims in international diplomacy but completely ignored them as far as India and other Asian and African colonies were concerned.

As I walked the length of the Tottenham Court Road, I tried to imagine stood that the shorting range here somewhere more than a hundred years ago, where this young man having bought a licensed Colt pistol from an arms dealer, now long gone, in nearby Holborn used to come every week to practise his shooting skills.

It was a London summer's day when this young man, whose entire life with all its possibilities open before him, a man who had already got his education from London and could have easily lived a life of comfort as his other colleagues, left his lodgings for the last time. He went to a public function to put his shooting skills to test. He was an educated man, who knew very well that his solitary act of revolutionary violence would not have immediately led to anything. The British Empire was at the peak of its power, the two World Wars were still to come, and the white man's imperialism of Asia and of Africa was the unchallenged norm of the times. But still on that day, the first of July, this young man shot and killed the then aide-de-camp (ADC) to the secretary of state for India, Curzon Wyllie. He was promptly arrested. Neither did he try to escape nor was there any possibility, and after a few days of trial that lasted hardly a day, where the young man had no defence counsel, he was convicted and sentenced to death. The trial took place at the Old Bailey, the criminal courts, that still stands today at the same spot.

The young man made a statement in court, justifying his actions as the only course open to a people of an oppressed nation against an aggressor. Drawing a comparison, he asked whether a British man would not have done the same and be considered a patriot were Germany to invade Britain? His case, as far as law was concerned, was doomed to being with, as he well knew, and he was sent to prison at Pentonville.

As one walks to the Pentonville prison, situated on Caledonian Road, not very far from the international railway station of St Pancras one is reminded of the horrific and violent past attached to it. Even today when executions are almost unimaginable, it is not very difficult to imagine that this forbidding-looking white building with its centuries old walls, that today houses petty criminals, was the final resting place of many. It was the place where, in that summer of 1909, the young man, disowned by his own family and the respectable leaders of his country, both of whom might have feared the consequences of associating with their wayward son, was hanged and, despite being known to be Hindu, was buried inside the prison with no religious rites.

Even today, there is no sign anywhere in London, with its numerous blue plaques commemorating the many worthy men and women who have lived here, that this young man ever lived and died here, miles away from his beloved motherland.

Madan Lal Dhingra—such was the young man's name, never worked with any expectation that he would be remembered by a grateful nation. A hundred years after his death, it is not for him, but for India's own sake and for the sake of its future that India should remember him and his sacrifice.

A Walk with Roald Dahl

It was at Universal Booksellers, Lucknow, while glancing through books by Roald Dahl that I came across the existence of a museum dedicated to this great writer of children's books. It was located in the village of Great Missenden in the county of Buckinghamshire in England. I had wished to visit it, being a fan. So, on a cold, dark, bleak and wet day, in short on a usual London day, we boarded the train from the century-old, quaint railway station of Marylebone, in London. But if Marylebone Station looked quaintly Victorian, the railway station at Great Missenden, where we got down after a short but beautiful train ride through the gently sloping Chiltern Hills, was frozen in time. The village, where the great writer was content to live for the last thirty-six years of his life, was, despite the occasional modern car, a proverbial English village, taken straight out of a Thomas Hardy or a Jane Austen novel, with its single street, a medieval church on a hilltop, a river running alongside the village, sloping hills and rolling farms all around.

A short walk down the only street, past the village library which Roald Dahl used to visit, past Dahl's favourite butcher's shop, past the ancient petrol pump and past the much more recent Indian 'curry house', brought us to the museum. The museum, although accommodated in barely half a dozen rooms, is curated with so much care that it informs, educates and entertains at the same time. It brings alive the author and his life through exhibits from his daily life, video and audio recordings, biographical narratives, manuscripts and photographs. But the 'jewel in the crown' is the immaculately reconstructed 'hut', as Dahl used to call his single-room cottage, built in the gardens of his house for him to write, complete with his chair, pencils and writing pads that he used to import from the US, his idiosyncratic collections, his ancient table lamp, heaters and even the dust on the carpet. It was to this hut that Dahl used to retreat every day for hours, as writing was lonely and hard work.

From the museum, we took a walk on an idyllic village trail, where Roald Dahl used to walk his children and later his grandchildren, to the medieval church where the grave of the famous author lay in the shade of a tree in the churchyard. Fans of his *Charlie and the Chocolate Factory*, *Matilda*, and *Going Solo* still come to pay their respects from all parts of the world. As we stood near the grave with its inscriptions on a black granite slab, the sun glanced through the clouds for the first time in the day, and the entire village below was awash with a brilliant light as if the heavens themselves were blessing us. That is the enduring memory of the village of Great Missenden that will remain with me.

Remembering the Poet Robert Burns and his Universal Humanism

2 5 January is Robert Burns's birth anniversary. In my childhood and youth, not as well, Burns was known to us in India as, say, Wordsworth, Keats or Shelley, and although I had heard the tunes of his immortal 'Auld Lang Syne' in some military parades, I didn't bother to understand the lyrics. But Robert Burns is not only the national poet of Scotland but also probably the most admired Scot, even more than two centuries after his death at the young and promising age of thirty-seven.

So on the 24 January, a day before, we walked to the banks of the Thames, where, in Victoria Embankment Gardens, a short wreath-laying ceremony had been arranged by the Burns Club of London. Over the years, numerous such clubs have sprung up all over the English-speaking world to commemorate Burns. There, at the feet of a monumental statue of the poet, his enthusiastic fans conducted a soulful yet austere programme, which started with a bagpiper procession and consisted of amateur but heartfelt renditions of his poetry. Among them was 'A Man is a Man', possibly his greatest piece, which speaks about the universal equality of all men, written in a world that was so class-ridden and unequal. A small but beautiful wreath was laid at the feet of the great poet before the final song of 'Auld Lang Syne' was sung—an ode to old times and friendships that touches the heart of every man and woman all over the world even today.

Sometimes I think that the appeal of great poets and writers—like Burns or Dickens or Tolstoy, or our own Tagore or Premchand or Manto—survived years and generations, because their universal humanism, empathy and timeless values make them truly great.

'Burns suppers' are organized by clubs and restaurants all over Scotland and England on the evening of his birth anniversary, and the traditional Scottish dish Haggis is enjoyed along with the inevitable scotch. Bagpiper music is played to which people attired in traditional Scottish attire dance energetically, after a customary recital of Burn's poetry, including his famous 'An Ode to Haggis'.

As a matter of fact, alongside his universal appeal, Robert Burns has also grown over the years to become a symbol of Scottish nationalism, as a kind Scottish gentleman, a former president of the Burns Club of London, explained to me. That nationalism may lead to a separate country of Scotland before long when it votes again on the referendum on this issue, but to me, Burn's words, travelling across tumultuous centuries past, across the artificial boundaries created by men, speaks to every man in every country who believes in the essential unity and equality of all men—'A man is a man and all that!'

Face-to-Face with Mahatma Gandhi in London

Gordon Square and Tavistock Square are two beautifully maintained public gardens, situated adjacent to each other and very close to the University Of London. The two are almost identical in their dimensions and are also similar, at least to my eyes, as far as the façades of the surrounding buildings go. But what is more remarkable about their similarity is that they have a statue each honouring a great Indian. A bust of Rabindranath Tagore adorns the centre of Gordon Square, while barely two hundred yards away is a lifelike statue of Mahatma Gandhi, depicting his usual bare-bodied self in his familiar cross-legged sitting posture, eyes almost closed meditatively, in Tavistock Square. It is really quite remarkable that these two of the greatest sons of India, who were not only contemporaries but also shared a close relationship based on deep mutual respect that rose over disagreements in views, should today adorn two adjacent squares in the heart of London—the capital of the same British Empire they fought against, albeit in their own manner.

It is hard to describe the feelings I had when I crossed Tavistock Square while walking to my daughter's school one morning and came face to face with the father of our nation, for the first time. I have seen statues and memorials to Gandhiji in foreign lands before—one in a well-maintained and well-located park in Geneva on the banks of Lake Geneva and another engraving at the UNESCO headquarters in Paris, and each time I felt pride and joy. But coming face to face with Gandhiji in the centre of Tavistock Square on that cloudy Monday morning in the heart of central London was different, maybe because of its total unexpectedness.

Later I realized that this particular statue of Gandhiji is quite well-known in London and it was here that the Indian high commissioner, on behalf of the government of India, pays homage on 2 October every year. When I crossed Gandhiji on 2 October, it was afternoon. There were a number of flower bouquets on his lap and below on the footsteps. Later, quite inexplicably, I found the bouquets, now with old and shrivelled flowers, lying there for days to come. This impressive statue is quite old unlike the bust of Tagore in Gordon Square, which was unveiled only in 2011. The statue of Bapu was unveiled as early as in 1968, barely two decades after our independence and after his demise, and was unveiled by no less than the then British Prime Minister, Harold Wilson. I wonder what Winston Churchill's reaction must have been to this blasphemous act of homage being paid by Her Majesty's government to that 'seditious lawyer acting as fakir'.

Very near the statue, inside Tavistock Square, stands a tree, a former version of which was planted by the then Indian prime minister and Gandhiji's disciple, Pandit Jawaharlal

Nehru, as a token of appreciation for the decision of the local council to have Gandhiji's statue in Tavistock Square. And the decision was quite appropriate too as Gandhiji, during his stay in London as a student of law in the last decades of the nineteenth century, must have visited the nearby University Law College for his lessons. Incidentally, Tagore too enrolled himself for the same course in law but never finished it. Apparently the Bar's loss was the gain of his numerous readers world over. It was difficult for me to imagine Gandhiji, then a young man barely in his twenties, dressed in Western clothes, coming to College all the way from Bromley, where he lived on chilly and cloudy winter days, at a time when there were no buses or electric street lights, when rigid Victorian social mores and distinctions still ruled the roost and an Indian in London was still a rarity. He might have also, in all probability, visited the imposing building of Tavistock House nearby, which used to be the home of the Theosophical Society, where he might have heard discourses on the Bhagvat Gita and other texts of ancient Hindu religion and which is the headquarters of the British Medical Association (BMA) today.

He must have felt the pain of Indian students who—having come all the way from the distant Indian subcontinent to live in the outskirts of London, having to commute to the colleges situated at its heart—were almost always famished, living on subsistence meals because of not only the high costs of living but also the bland food that their English landladies would prepare. It must have been a common ordeal for many Indian students then, as I suspect it must be now, but Gandhiji later did something to ease the situation, and it was mainly on his advice and inspiration that the YMCA (Young Men's Christian Association) India would later open a hostel for Indian students—now appropriately named after Gandhiji—which still runs in nearby Fitzroy Square, at the heart of University area of London. It continues to do an immense service to students from India, who get a place to stay at a reasonable cost and get wholesome Indian food and the long-missed familiarity of an Indian atmosphere.

As I walked around Tavistock Square, it appeared to me that the local council (in London it is called a 'borough'), the Council of Camden, was quite committed, at least in appearance, to the values of peace, humanity, equality and anti-racism. Apart from the statue of the apostle of peace himself, which is the real 'jewel in the crown' of the park, there was a cherry tree for the remembrance of the victims of the atomic bombs dropped on the Japanese cities of Hiroshima and Nagasaki in 1945. I also learnt about Dr Nirmal Roy, definitely a man of Indian origin, who had become the mayor of the Camden Council and in whose memory a tree had been planted in Tavistock Square with a plaque that commemorates his lifelong commitment to the values of 'non-violence, anti-apartheid and anti-racism'. In a way, the entire atmosphere in Tavistock Square, with all its memorials and trees, appeared to be a humble homage to the great father of Indian nation and his values, who even today attracts the respect and wonder of people from all walks of life and all nationalities.

On many an evening, I would feel happy to see a father, and not always from the Indian subcontinent, pointing towards the statue of Gandhiji and telling his son or daughter something about the values that the Mahatma stood for. It appeared to me that maybe that is the real value of all statues and all memorials everywhere.

A Sunny Spring Weekend in London

Weekends anywhere, at least in any big city of the world where the majority of its inhabitants go to work every weekday, are always cherished. But if it is a sunny weekend in spring, London becomes truly special, when shafts of sunlight play through the new leaves of plane, ash, chestnut and maple trees and when the bluebells in the manicured flower beds sway in the gentle breeze, after the long hiatus of the dark and gloomy winter months.

The touristy parks and squares of central London was still full of local residents and students, basking in the sun, drinking beer or eating ice cream sold by vendors from their old-fashioned vans. As I sat on the green lawns of Russell Square, shading my eyes from the rays of sun filtering through the tree branches and looking at the gaiety all around me, the fountains suddenly awakened for the first time after months of winter.

I realized that, once upon another spring day, Charles Dickens may have sat here, as he used to live quite nearby, perhaps thinking about the plot of *Hard Times* or perhaps thinking of the tumultuous and secret love of his life. The fountains would not have been here in Dickens's time nor when T.S. Eliot worked for years together in his nearby office of Faber & Faber and lived through a painful *Wasteland* of a marriage. Perhaps, I thought, it was in one such hope-filled sunny spring weekend morning that Eliot decided to marry his secretary, whom he had loved for years. It was difficult to imagine, but it was true that, almost during the same decades, when Eliot was working here, W.B. Yeats lived barely two hundred yards away. I wondered what Yeats's landlady might have made of her tenant before and after he became world famous and won the Noble Prize for Literature.

Many of the buildings that I saw all around me were not that old, having been constructed after their predecessors were bombed during World War II. One such building was the nearby Tavistock Hotel, where Virginia and Leonard Woolf's house and publishing company Hogarth Press, used to be and where Virginia Woolf's famous or infamous friends used to come together, provoking London society to call them the 'Bloomsbury group', with all its connotations.

Incidentally, nowhere in Bloomsbury did I find a bust, let alone a statue, of Charles Dickens or of W.B. Yeats, of T.S. Eliot or George Orwell. There was a solitary, almost hidden bust of Virginia Woolf in an almost hidden corner of Tavistock Square. But right at the centre of Russell Square stood the grand bronze statue of one of the Dukes of Bedford, whose family owned all the land around for centuries. Today nobody remembers him, but the words of Dickens and Orwell travel every day, across miles and centuries, to ordinary people like me.

But London is not only about literature, culture and history. It is but also a symbol of the wealth and riches that were made to flow into it for centuries—from distant India, China, Africa and the Caribbean; from the profits generated through slave trade and the 'acquisitions' made in Greece and Egypt that London's museums are filled with. But perhaps today, Londoners want to move on with their lives, with the worries of jobs and bills, of taxes and pensions crowding out any other thought from their minds.

Away from the parks, inside a residential area, spotted an old London gentleman, having a leisurely roast and ale, reading *The Guardian* in a pub. I wondered what his thoughts were when he looked at the London of today, a London that had since his youth gone through the Thatcherite years of privatization and globalization. I felt, today's London was definitely far more clean and perhaps more prosperous than the days when he up had grown but then one's impressions and memories rely rarely on just facts. There are millions of Londons, each different for and unique to every one of its residents, and what I see may not be the same as what he sees.

Today London is much more diverse and multicultural than perhaps seventy years ago. People from all over the world—East Europeans, French, Africans, South Asians, Chinese, et al. visit and live in London. Immigration is a major issue in politics and TV debates, as it has been for years and almost everywhere in the rich, 'First' World, where the economic logic clashes every day with fears, emotions and insecurities.

The old gentleman finished his ale, and donning his Yorkshire cap, got up to ready himself for the coming week. The sun had set, the birds had flown back to their invisible nests, and another London weekend had come to an inevitable end.

Meeting Lucknow in London

London appears, at least to most Indians, a distant, exotic place, somewhere across the seven seas as it was in the days of the East India Company. But India does not seem to be so far away in London. Mostly because everywhere one walks in London one comes across people of Indian origin, and here I mean Indians, Pakistanis and Bangladeshis all together, as it is very difficult to distinguish one from the other. These may be people who have been living in London for generations or students who have come to study in London barely a few months back or even tourists, as the Indian middle class increases in volume as well as in aspirations. Also, although the modern Britisher does not like to remind himself too often of the defunct British Empire, reminders of that past are always lurking around the corner. From the painting depicting the Siege of Lucknow at the National Portrait Gallery to the statues of Robert Clive next to St James Park, to the busts of Indian heroes like Tagore, Gandhi and Nehru, to the rooms at Bedford Square where Raja Ram Mohan Roy lived during his stay in

London or where Sir Syed lived, where the guest house of the Goodenough College stands today—all remind us of a past that remains as a part of our collective mutual existence.

Remarkably, the first time I met someone from Lucknow in London was barely a couple of days after we had arrived. I met them at a welcome tea arranged thoughtfully at the university hall in the campus where we lived. The gentleman, grey, very fair and distinguished-looking in a Western sort of way, accompanied by his Australian wife and daughter, whom he had come to get settled, seemed at first to belong to the First World. But that was before he introduced himself to us. He was born in Lucknow, in Narhi, barely a couple of kilometres away from where we live, but decades ago in British India. His father, who worked in the Forest Service, later migrated to Lahore in the uncertain aftermath of the Partition and he himself had grown up and had graduated from the Medical College in Lahore—an equivalent to our own King George Medical College (KGMC). He was now living in Adelaide with his Australian wife. Nevertheless, even after six decades, he distinctly recalled the Lucknow of his childhood—Narhi, Hazratganj and Banarasi Bagh. As he recounted, I was reminded of *Sunlight on a Broken Column* by Attia Hosain—a brilliant novel by that proud daughter of Lucknow, who too was forced to leave her hometown because of a twist in history.

Since then I met other people from Lucknow: a financier who had been living in London for the past four decades along with his wife from Turin; a doctor from KGMC who had been living in Dover for as many years; a young doctor couple, once from La Marts, who were living in London for the past few years and had not yet decided about the future;

a young professional and mother who worked from British Telecom. The one thing I found common in all of them was that, though they had left Lucknow, Lucknow had not left them. The images of the silhouette of Chattar Manzil against the evening sky, the banks of the Gomti, the pavements of Hazratganj and the lanes of Aminabad keep coming back to their minds, and they remain Lucknowites, even after decades!

Bristol! Bristol!

Sometimes I travel to a place with lots of ideas and expectations after having read and heard about it from various sources, and then end up feeling disappointed, maybe because of the raised expectations. This is what happened with me, for example, when I visited the city of Bath, a tourist hotspot as well as an almost universally recommended place to visit. I don't blame Bath for my disappointment as the interaction between a traveller and a place depends on both parties. But Bristol, not very far from Bath, was the exact opposite, because I didn't have too many expectations from it and had decided to travel to the city more as a means of 'filling up' one of my London weekends, before finally embarking on my long journey home. But as it turned out, it was one of the most pleasant days I had spent in England, and there was something in the air, in the light, in the fragrance, in the sky and the clouds, in the greens and the flower beds, or maybe there was something inside me that day that made the day so beautiful.

England on a bright summer day, especially in the countryside, can be very beautiful—and how beautiful it can be I realize once again on that journey that morning to Bristol. I normally prefer travelling by train, and something about the moving frames of the wide windows and the unique rambling sound of the wheels on the steel rails make me enthusiastic and nostalgic at the same time. Nevertheless I decided to board a highway coach to Bristol instead of embarking on a journey on the 150-year-old Paddington–Bristol railway line that owes its existence to that legendary British engineer Brunel, one of the most respected and revered personalities of all time almost anywhere in England but especially in Bristol.

Sometimes hitting the road is also fun, and on that Sunday morning, as my coach glided west on the smooth highway that runs through the gently sloping, green countryside of middle England, past the urban sprawls of Greater London, the much anticipated monotony of the scene provided me with a sense of comfort and stability—nothing spectacular, no particular sights to see, just endless green fields and meadows, occasional country house and village churches with its spires rising like fountains. This was the same highway on which I had travelled earlier during my journeys to Cardiff and to Bath, but every road, every highway, even every street and lane in a city, anywhere in the world, keeps much hidden in its bosom for the traveller to unravel.

As the quintessential English countryside rolled by the windows of my coach, the travels of an Englishman on an oriental highway came to mind as I was reading Rob Gifford's *China Road*, and somehow the two journeys seemed to merge into one. But the countryside outside was spectacularly empty of people—there were no farmers, no agricultural activities, no signs of Sunday mass at the village churches, and I wondered who lived in these centuries old villages and what filled up their lives. However, it was not too long a journey, and before the sun reached its zenith, the coach was easing itself into the coach station at Bristol.

Bristol's heyday lay in England's mercantile medieval period. Bristol's dockyards on the Atlantic Ocean provided it with maritime prosperity, and along with York in the north, it was—after London—the most important city in England. Later, during the Industrial Revolution, it missed the bus and was overtaken by the northern industrial cities of Manchester and Liverpool, perhaps because of their proximity to the coal mines. But today, post-maritime days, post-industrial days, post-colonial days, Bristol is once again reinventing itself through tourism and higher education—two of the industries that are very important to modern England.

Bristol's maritime prosperity depended to a considerable measure on a peculiar and inhuman trade that would and, in my opinion, should remain etched in the collective consciousness of mankind. Huge ships laden with manufactured products used to set sail on a triangular journey from the dockyards of Bristol to destinations in Western Africa. There, this cargo was exchanged for African men and women, who were taken in appallingly inhuman conditions on the long and dangerous journey across the Atlantic Ocean to the Americas as slaves, so that they could fulfil the labour needs of the farms in the newly 'settled' lands, which in turn had been created by an almost complete annihilation of native races. The ships loaded farm produce like cotton and corn from America and brought it back to Bristol along with those of the crew who were fortunate enough to have survived, plus a few Africans who would spent the rest of their lives working as household servants in the country mansions of English aristocrats.

Slave trade was legally abolished in 1807, but of course the demand for slaves kept the trade alive, even if illegally, for years afterwards. As I walked up Corn Street and the empty lanes of Nicholson Market, I felt that perhaps the prosperity and grandeur of the Bath stone façade mansions and buildings owed much to the blood and sweat, to the tears and corpses of those unfortunate people from African villages who lay in those bulging hulks of ships that embarked from the harbour side nearby. True, one can't change history, but one should never forget history, either.

In front of the huge façade of the 'corn exchange' buildings stands four squat steel pillars called 'nails', where monetary deals were struck between local merchants, and in the 'commercial rooms' nearby, today a pub perhaps, stood the offices of those merchants. Those merchants, in those dark and grey Georgian times, in the days before the steam engine, before the railways, before the electric light, in the days of Edmund Burke—who was a local member of Parliament and during the battles of Plassey and Buxar in a distant land, must have walked over the same cobblestoned lanes. Corn Street, the harbour side, Nicholson Market, the cathedral nearby—all stood then and were witnesses to all that happened there in those auction houses, in the coach stations, in the public houses. If only they could speak, I wondered—how different the history that we read today would have been.

The real reason for my decision to travel to Bristol that Sunday was that I wanted to visit the place where, perhaps the first really great modern Indian, Raja Ram Mohan Roy, breathed his last in 1830. The great social reformer and scholar, considered by many as one of the founding fathers of Indian Renaissance, had created a unique synthesis of Western ideas and traditional Indian thought based on ancient texts. I knew from my readings that he had embarked on the long sea voyage from then Calcutta (now Kolkata) to England, a taboo for Hindus in those days. He had sailed to mainly represent the legal case of the Nawabs of Awadh to the British government and the Crown as the Nawab had no longer any faith in the officials of the East India Company in India. He stayed in Bedford Square in central London during his stay. Nevertheless, what took him further on the long journey to Bristol, I cannot say. Perhaps he went there simply to board a ship and to sail back home. Ships, in those pre-Suez Canal days, would have sailed around the Cape of Good Hope to India, and Bristol would have been the natural sailing port.

I wondered what the thoughts going through the mind of the great man had been as he lay on his deathbed in Bristol, thousands of miles away from his homeland, and what impression his experiences of England and the West had made on his mind. I wished he had written a journal about his last days in England. Perhaps he did, and maybe someday in the future, his diaries, like the diaries of Samuel Pepys, would be discovered in some lost cabinet or box in some long-forgotten room or attic in Bristol. A few years ago, a larger-than-life statue of Raja Ram Mohan Roy had been put up in the heart of the city, just in front of Bristol Cathedral, and the nobility of the sculpture is matched by its prominent location, an indication of the man's greatness and Bristol's acknowledgement of the same. I could notice old British ladies and curious tourists stopping to gaze at the impressive statue and to read the plaque underneath that described him.

Nowhere in Britain is India far-off, and if the statue of Raja Ram Mohan Roy pointed to how the historical legacies of the two countries are interwoven, restaurants with names like 'Chandni Chowk' in the heart of Park Road, or taxi drivers from the Indian subcontinent who work on the streets of Bristol, pointed to how the Indian subcontinent remains so much a part of present-day Britain. But, increasingly, immigrants from India have moved up the skill chain, and recent immigration from India is more likely to be of highly skilled professionals, academics or even entrepreneurs, unlike a couple of decades ago. Whether there is a definite pattern in this or whether one can draw any conclusion from it is difficult to say, but I feel, after a stay of almost one year in London, that it does have a rhythm.

Later as the sun moved across the clear blue sky, I wandered to the leafy and green Brendon Hill and climbed up the narrow steps of Cabot Tower—a tower that had been erected more than a century ago to commemorate the fourth centenary of the voyage of Cabot, a Bristolian, to North America. The tower, situated on top of the hill, affords an excellent vantage point of not only the city sprawled below but also the distant rolling countryside, merging into the hazy horizon like the waves of a sea, as a whiff of a fresh, crisp breeze blows on one's face. But definitely, the two most attractive sights from atop Cabot Tower are both creations of that remarkable man Brunel—the *SS Britain* docked at Bristol, the first steamship to cross the Atlantic and now a museum, and the even more impressive Clifton Bridge, the huge steel and girder, suspension bridge that has been spanning Avon Gorge for more than one-and-a-half centuries. My first view of Clifton Bridge immediately brought to mind the numerous photographs and pictures of various other suspension bridges from all over the world—Golden Gate Bridge in San Francisco, Chain Bridge in Budapest and even our own Howrah Bridge in Kolkata, all of which can trace their origin, directly or indirectly, to the massive engineering marvel that glitters in the night as the sun sets over Bristol.

Through in Bristol the greed and cruelty of man took shape in the form of the inhuman slave trade, it was here too that great human minds erected Clifton Bridge and embarked on remarkable human endeavours. In Bristol, as in everywhere else, the human mind and heart shows impossible heights and equally unfathomable depths.

As I stood on Brunel's great bridge and gazed at the surrounding Forest of Avon and the gorge below, with Bristol lying a little distance away, I could see a procession of centuries walking along the streets and harbour side: merchants in black top hats, orators like Edmund Burke, uncouth shouts in the corn exchanges, deeds of greedy merchants, pubs and taverns overflowing with sailors, a Brunel goading his labourers on, a saintly Raja Ram Mohan Roy despairing over his enslaved motherland and a solitary black man weeping in some corner of a cellar in the house of a Georgian gentleman.

In the Footsteps of William Wordsworth

William Wordsworth, when he lived in the sleepy and beautiful little village of Grasmere, would have perforce walked all the way to the shores of Lake Windermere to catch a steam ferry to travel across. The ferry, though no longer operating on steam, still runs back and forth dutifully with its tell-tale sound of blaring horns, a throwback to another age. Looking at it, I was reminded of another time, another place—pre-partition Bengal of my father's childhood, when such scheduled ferry services, operating on the mighty waterways of the Ganges Delta, were the principal means of transport. Nowadays, just like in Lake Windermere, a solitary ferry service crossing the River Hoogly in Kolkata is a reminder of those days, gone forever.

Today, of course, there is an excellent highway that connects the ferry point to the village of Grasmere, and we boarded a rather touristy open-top bus, No. 599, that trundled up through the twin villages of Bowness and Windermere. The green hills, or 'fells' as they are called, and their grassy slopes on one side and the occasional tantalizing glimpse of the grey–blue surface of the lake, sparkling under the sun, on the other made the ride especially beautiful. Although we were passing through rather touristy villages like Ambleside and Brockhole that were full of cafés and souvenir shops, with crowds of tourists and mountain walkers enjoying the Bank Holiday weekend, there were reminders of another age in the stone bell tower of the village church and the ancient clock that adorned the façade of the town hall that used to triple up as a courtroom and a prison.

I like to venture into the cool and spacious interiors of a solitary village church, away from the tourist trail, not only because it affords a rare oasis of peace, contemplation and solitude, even in the busiest tourist deluge, but also because the plaques and paintings that adorn the walls, as also the churchyard itself, tells the story of the village and of how the church used to be central to the fears and festivities of the villagers. The dark, spacious and yet friendly interiors of the Church of St Mary were also remarkable because of the giant in situ mural that covered one of its walls. It was as exquisite as it was unexpected. It was painted during World War II by a student of the Royal Academy of Arts after that institution had been relocated from London to nearby Ambleside to escape the German Blitz.

The huge mural depicts a village ceremony, tracing its origin to some obscure medieval past—part religious and part social and part unique to the parish. Although at the time of my visit the church was quite deserted, it had been lovingly maintained, and the altar, the shining organ, the baptistery, the pulpit and even the pews showed that the church was still important in the lives of the villagers.

Even without its famous association with William Wordsworth, Grasmere would still be an exquisite, gem of a village standing on the shores of Lake Grasmere. At the centre of the village is the medieval church in the grounds of which rest the graves, in the shade of a tree planted by the poet himself, of Wordsworth's family. Nearby stands a small building that housed the poet's school once, and from where, today, the famous Sarah Nelson's gingerbread is sold like hot cakes. Perhaps, I wondered, the exquisite views—the surrounding green hills, the shimmering lake, the sleepy mountain trails and the woods that stretched up to distant horizon—had attracted the poet to settle down and make his home in this village.

Today, such gentle beauty is somewhat lost on the modern tourist, anxious as he is to reach the widely publicized Dove Cottage—the small cottage where Wordsworth lived for a decade or so, first with his adoring sister, Dorothy and later, in addition, with his wife and a rapidly growing brood of children. For more than a century now, the cottage has been lovingly preserved as a memorial and attracts tourists, lovers of poetry, students and researchers from all over the world. It was a pleasant surprise to find a family from Kolkata, of all places in the world, along with us. For them, the visit had been a lifelong dream—to visit their childhood hero who had opened their minds eye's to the imagined beauty of daffodils in a land of magnolias and marigolds. There were many Japanese tourists too, as a special exhibition had been mounted based on the works of a famous Japanese illustrator in the same premises.

Dove Cottage to me is not only a memorial to a great poet but also a valuable and faithful picture of another age, an age when Queen Victoria was yet to ascend the throne of England, an age when steam locomotives had not yet reached Lake District, an age when automobiles and electricity were not even imagined and the only means to reach the beautiful but distant village was to walk or use a horse carriage. Perhaps that was how Wordsworth's friends the famous poets Samuel Coleridge, Robert Southy or Walter Scott—would have reached Dove Cottage at the end of a day of tiring hike. And knocking at the very same door that stood before me, they would have been let in by a smiling Dorothy into the warmth of a home warmed by the very same fireplace that was before me.

The beautiful commentary of the elderly volunteer guide brought Dove Cottage to life, and I could almost see a young Dorothy writing in her journal in the light of a lamp or tending to the beautiful garden outside, as a young William returned from a walk in the hills to pen down one of his poems on nature. Like all truly great poets, Wordsworth's greatness lay not only in his exquisite poetry, beautiful as it undoubtedly is, but also in his indelible imprint and influence on generations of later poets—Keats, Shelley, Byron et al—and other poets outside of his native land and his native language.

Later as the great poet's family and fortunes grew, the cottage was found to be insufficient, and they shifted to the nearby village of Rydal, settling into a bigger house called Rydal Mount, not to be confused with the nearby Rydal Hall. This house, unlike Dove Cottage, is still owned, maintained and run as a museum by the descendants of the poet. The garden surrounding the house is even more beautiful than the house itself, and the view that it affords—folds upon folds of distant hills gently sloping down to the still water, the sounds of birds chirping, rows of flowers swaying in a gentle breeze, the candy floss white clouds in a clear blue sky above—must have inspired the poet not only to produce those infinitely beautiful pieces of poetry but also to continue living here, even after he had become famous and been honoured as Poet Laureate. But the same house that inspired him so much and was witness to his great creations was also the place that brought infinite pain to his heart when he lost his most loved daughter, Dora, here, in one of the rooms upstairs. Wordsworth, people say, was not the same man, ever since—a poignant and sad reminder of the mortality of man and his happiness.

I walked back to Windermere, over a beautifully marked footpath, over swaying wooden bridges that spanned gently flowing streams, through farmlands where sheep grazed contently, through woods dark and deep. I was somehow reminded of a walk that I had taken long ago from Nainital to Kimberley. Who knows, maybe a century ago, an Englishman walking that same distant mountain path in the foothills of the Himalayas might have been reminded of his native Lake District. Maybe that is how places travel over oceans and across centuries and how a New 'York' is settled on another continent, a Christ Church is built in distant Lucknow and a Lucknow takes shape on the shores of a distant lake in Canada!

A Bright Day in Brighton

There was a time when Brighton was a small, sleepy, isolated seaside village in the southern coast of England. As is so often the case in England, Brighton's first claim to fame arose when royalty bestowed its grace upon it: The Prince Regent, later King George IV, chose Brighton as the place to indulge in a dalliance with his then lady love. However, it was with the advent of the railway line from London that Brighton really transformed into a day-trip destination for Londoners and tourists and gained its reputation as a fun destination, with a trace of Bohemianism that it retains to this day.

Although the day itself was bright and blue, summer had long gone when we boarded a coach from London to Brighton one weekend. Intercity buses are called coaches in Britain; the long-forgotten-horse, drawn coaches were used for intercity travel, and the name lingers on.

The National Express Coach that we took ends its journey at a shelter with absolutely no facilities, but has an excellent location. One can just saunter across the road to the beach, with the Brighton Pier right in front.

Right at the entrance of the pier stood a recently installed Ferris wheel, something like a Brighton Eye (similar to the London Eye). Then there were temporary stalls from where you could pick up gear and a guide to go bungee jumping. There was an excited crowd of kids shrieking. Amidst a slight and short-lived drizzle, we walked into the long, extended, brightly decorated and yet a century-old Brighton Pier, full with roller coasters, carousels, game arcades, eateries, bars, cafés and ice-cream parlours and which extends right into the bluish grey waves of the Celtic Sea, with gulls hovering overhead amidst the sound of music from the live DJ. Attractive as the manmade attractions were, the most beautiful was the majestic sea in front of us, extending up to the distant horizon. There was no land in view, and only a couple of distant ships, small from where we were, floated across. On our right, only a few hundred yards away, stood the ruins of another Victorian Pier that must one day have been as bright and as gay; I was reminded of the famous poem 'Ozymandias' by Shelley. Unexpectedly we came across excellent freshly fried Bhature and Chole, prepared and being sold by a gentleman from Jalandhar, amidst the various pubs selling fish and chips and warm ales. As we walked along the extended beach of shingles, towards the Brighton Marina, I saw a sea-facing old Victorian hotel, proudly proclaiming that it was at that hotel that British Prime Minister Gladstone used to stay during his visits to Brighton.

Having once been an engineer, I was especially keen to travel on the world's oldest running electric train, the Voks

Railway, that an along the coast for some two miles or so, from Brighton Pier to the Marina. And we were lucky since it was the last weekend before the train was to stop running for the tourist-less winter months. More than a hundred years ago, Mr Voks started this electric train, and although the carriages had since been renovated a number of times, and the rails and signals might also have been, the historicity and a certain atmosphere of the railway line did come through. On one side, I could see twenty-first century vehicles whizzing past on the highway, facing which stood a series of Georgian and Victorian mansions, the playfields of the world's rich. On another side was the vast, muted, bluish grey, Celtic Sea.

Today it is difficult to imagine that this peaceful sea and these beaches were the site of intense barricading, mines and tension with aircrafts hovering overhead and radars watching the sky, as during World War II a German attack was expected. Brighton Pier lay abandoned for years; food was rationed; and fear and worry along with a desperate resolution, must have been writ large on the faces of parents and grandparents of today's residents.

Later in the afternoon, we walked to the Royal Pavilion—a curious Indo-Sarcenic building with Indian style domes and courtyards—designed by the Prince Regent's favourite architect and landscaper John Nash. Nevertheless, to compare it to the Taj Mahal, as some local brochures did, was ridiculous. The structure is impressive in itself, but when compared to the incomparable Taj, it would appear somewhat akin to the Mughal emperor's stables.

I noticed an elderly Sikh gentleman explaining the architecture of the building to his English friend. Perhaps he didn't know that thousands of Sikh solders from the same villages of Punjab from where he hailed were housed in the Royal Pavilion when it was converted into a military hospital for injured Indian soldiers during World War I.

As the sun set and a full moon arose over the silvery sea on a clear night, we set off on our return journey to London.

Across the Border to Wales

My earliest recollection of Wales is watching the Prince of Wales, Charles, marrying Lady Diana Spencer, an event which the British and the world media managed to project into an event of world importance. Only much later did I realize that Wales is a nation, different and separate from England, with as different a language as can be and a different culture—the difference depending on who you ask! So naturally, I was keen to avail of the opportunity to visit Cardiff, the capital city of Wales, when it presented itself. It was an organized day-long bus trip, mainly aimed at university students and started near Victoria Station in London. Most of our fellow passengers seemed to be international students—Turks, Pakistanis, Eastern European and Mediterranean, and there was a virtual Tower of Babel inside the bus.

It was a longish bus journey towards the west, mainly through straight highways flanked by rolling countrysides, with the sun playing hide, and, seek among intermittent clouds. After some time, past the diversion to the city of Bristol, we suddenly found that the sign on the highway was written in two languages: one in familiar English but another that had only the script in common, with a lot of 'y's and 'w's in every word. I guessed that we must have crossed the border and entered Wales.

Although Wales is reputed to be more close to nature, with hills and forests, at least compared to the more urbanized England, Cardiff is like any other big, international city in the Western world—eminently comfortable, rich, smooth and cultural in a very expected sort of way. Everyone who visits Cardiff spends a considerable time at Cardiff Castle, the ruins of a medieval castle now presented, marketed and packaged to tourists. As we walked past the old stone walls of the castle, I noticed remarkable statues of animals, erected on top of the wall and made as if for a class of zoology students. The streets and lanes of Cardiff that day were full of Welsh rugby fans, in colourful t-shirts and headgear with red dragons painted on them, with beer cans in hand, preparing to shout for the Rugby World Cup's big match between Wales and Argentina in a few hours. We could see the bulge of the stadium on the banks of a muddy river, which skirted the castle and flowed into the Celtic Sea, providing an alternative route for tourists to reach the sea—coast on motor boats.

Following the creation of the Cardiff Bay Barrage in the nineties, the old marina became a manmade lake, but it was still a pleasant enough stroll along the waterfront. Impressive modern buildings like that of the Welsh National Assembly along with the old dockyard offices of an era long gone presented an interesting backdrop. A Welsh boatman gave us a ride on his ancient motorboat, he pointed out and as the boat sputtering along the coast the different sights to us. There were precious few wild sea fowl, and we spotted a once-upon-a-time Norwegian church where the famous writer Roald Dahl was baptized. It has now been converted into a café. A cold and fierce wind was blowing against our faces, but the novel and exotic experience kept us interested. The Welsh boatman didn't seem to have too many Indian tourists but was quite familiar with India and Mumbai.

If India and Indians seemed to be distant in Cardiff as against London, the notion was soon dismissed when we went to the Wales National Museum later in the evening. It was sheer coincidence that on that very day of our visit, the local Indian community had organized a Diwali Mela at the Museum, although Diwali was long past. I could see sari-clad women with large bindis on their foreheads, who, though long separated from their motherland, were trying to stick to their culture in a foreign land, trying to maintain the umbilical cord that still bound them to India, across the seas, even after years.

Right in front of the Museum stood a life-size statue of David Lloyd George, the most famous son of Wales and one of the most admired and famous of all British prime ministers. He had lived, worked and embarked on his remarkable political career in Wales before moving to London to do greater things, including leading Britain to victory in World War I. At the rear of the statue, a Christmas fair, with German huts, stalls selling mulled wine, hamburgers, ice-creams and merry-go-round were in full swing, and despite the chill, families were milling around enjoying their last weekend before Christmas.

The sun had set by around 4.30 to 5.00 p.m., and the air was nippy when we found ourselves and our fellow passengers congregating in our coach. We were so keen on seeing the sights of Cardiff and absorbing the atmosphere of Wales that we, all of us, had forgotten to interact with our fellow passengers from various national and cultural groups—one of the advantages of such group journeys. But now it was too late and everyone was too tired. The coach drove us back across the dark countryside and through the highways full of rush-hour traffic and rugby fans returning home.

It was a nice trip, on expected lines, without anything spectacular, but then maybe Cardiff, despite being the capital, is not really representative of Wales, a Wales of wild interiors, forests, hills and natural beauty. So I returned with a feeling that I must return to Wales again, maybe to the Snowdonia Hills or to the national parks to get a more definitive impression of what Wales is. Till then, I bid adieu to Wales as the highway sign became familiar once more, and we returned to England, across the invisible border.

On Hovercraft across the English Channel

Britain itself is an island, but apart from the mainland, it has a number of smaller 'isles' scattered around, and the two most famous among them are the Isle of Wight on the Solent to the south and the Isle of Man on the Irish Sea to the west, and that is pretty much what the once mighty British Empire, where the sun never set, has been reduced to, thankfully.

Apart from being the most convenient getaway to the Isle of Wight, the city of Portsmouth has a character and history of its own, and it was to Portsmouth that we took a bus trip to, on one of the weekends. The YMCA India, situated in central London, arranges such day trips thoughtfully for the benefit of its residents, but for also others like us, who are welcome to join. The bus journey, run by 'Dhillon of London', was nothing spectacular, although the countryside was beautiful, in a manicured sort of way. The bus dropped us right on the marina, and then everyone was to his own.

We took a leisurely walk along the coastline, past the Burj al Arab like Spinnaker Tower, through the historic naval area.

In centuries past, Portsmouth was, and to some extent still is, a very important port for the Royal Navy, and it was from here that ships sailed for India. It was from here that one day the warships of Admiral Nelson went off to thwart the invasion; and it was again, from here, on D-Day during World War II, that the invasion of Nazi-controlled continental Europe was mounted. The remnants of these historical events are carefully preserved and presented all along the historic naval area, with Nelson's ship *HMS Victory* looming large. However we walked past to the old ramparts and stone towers that lay on the turbulent sea coast. From there the grey Solent lay in front of us, reflecting the grey sky overhead and the mist obscuring the horizon. Salt water sprays drenched the ancient ramparts as the angry waves thrashed against them. It must have looked the same to countless sailors once, who would have bid their homeland adieu, some never to return, with their graves now resting somewhere in some foreign sea.

But it was the hovercraft ride to the Isle of Wight, across the Solent, that was our main goal. Portsmouth is the only place in Britain, and one of the few remaining in the world, from where you can take a commercial ride on a hovercraft. None of us had ever even seen a hovercraft, and it was quite spectacular to watch the giant amphibious craft climbing right on to the beach with its huge fan whirling behind. The novelty was the main feature of our short trip to the Isle of Wight, as we sat in our seats in a wide aircraft-like cabin, along with other eager tourists and equally nonchalant daily commuters. The Isle soon appeared through a grey curtain of mist, and we landed on the beach. It was through the same waters that Queen Victoria once sailed to her favourite haunt on the Isle, the Osborne House, where she used to escape to for peace, away from the politics and government of London. Today the Osborne House, where the Queen also found her final peace, is a public museum.

As is the case everywhere in England, there is always a connection with the Indian subcontinent somewhere, if only one strives to look. Here too, we found, one Bhai Ram Singh from Lahore, who, though long forgotten in his homeland, had helped design the Durbar Hall of Osborne House.[2] It shows not only the undoubted talents of Bhai Ram Singh but also the acceptance of the same by the British.

Our trip to the Isle of Wight was short—too short to do justice to the beautiful island—as we had to return to London the same day. We had to forgo a ride on the ancient steam locomotive that runs through the small island, and we returned late evening to Portsmouth on the same hovercraft. This time we sailed under a brilliant blue sky with white seagulls hovering overhead, but not before sampling a typical British meal of fish and chips, of Yorkshire pudding and mashed potatoes and peas, which like the hovercraft was remarkable for mainly its novelty.

I really wished that I had had the time to visit the birthplace of Charles Dickens, a house in Portsmouth that had been converted into a small museum, as I had lately started to enjoy his novels, both his masterly use of language and also, and even more, his remarkable empathy and humanism that

---

[2] He also designed Aitchison College, National College of Arts and the University of Punjab—all in Lahore, and many buildings in the erstwhile kingdoms of Patiala, Nabha, Jind, Jammu, and Kashmir.

can only come probably through 'living it himself'. Sir Arthur Conan Doyle, the doctor who created Sherlock Holmes, also lived in Portsmouth for some time when the absence of patients drew him to writing. Who knew what destiny had in store for any of us. Maybe, someday, my destiny would bring me back to the city of Portsmouth. And with these thoughts in my mind, my family and I got on to the bus to London, with a benevolent full moon accompanying us throughout, as our bus wound up through the now dark and distant countryside.

Museums and Galleries in London

One of the most attractive features of living in London is the prospect of visiting the numerous and well-stocked museums and galleries that not only are beautifully curated and preserved but also, barring exceptions, offer you free entry. 'When the weather is good, visit the parks and gardens; when the weather is bad, which is quite often, visit the museums and galleries' is a good rule of thumb for spending a free day in London, as we discovered very early during our stay.

Yes, one does feel sad and a bit offended to find Indian treasures displayed in a foreign capital; treasures that were 'acquired' by British officials, in their private capacities at the height of the colonial era—and the feeling is not lessened by the fact that, compared to India, there are far more artistic treasures from Greece, Turkey, Italy and Egypt on display. One feels sad not only because there was an era in our history when we were so weak and divided that a small and distant island nation could rule over such a vast, ancient land but also because, unlike some other countries like Greece, independent India has never really made a vocal or visible claim on these parts of our heritage. To say that one can't turn back the clock of history, to my mind, is for the British to say, not us.

Questions of their origin aside, it has to be admitted that the exhibits are beautifully and sensitively presented, and the commentaries illuminating them are, again, barring a few exceptions, balanced and devoid of any obvious colonial bias.

Not only in Britain but also across Europe, visiting museums and galleries is a major part of the leisure activities of even ordinary families, and so on every holiday I would find entire families of Londoners enjoying their visit to the British Museum along with the inevitable crowd of tourists from all over the world. School children, accompanied by their harassed teachers, would be trying to copy the masterpieces in the National Gallery along with professional artists and students from the Royal Academy of Arts or from the Slade School. I felt that this interest in their heritage, history and art had been built over generations, and with the weight of habit and socialization, it had become a part of the collective education of the society.

Every country, every city, every street in the world has a past, but to convert the present into tomorrow's history requires the written word, and that it is the historians, the chroniclers and the travellers. A Herodotus, a Strabo or a Gibbon have created histories as much as the kings and emperors whose stories they wrote. Elsewhere, there was neither the inclination nor the luxury to record history, as perhaps entire time and effort was spent on making two ends meet, on looking for the next meal, on protecting oneself and one's family from marauding armies. So it was the words of the Rosetta Stone that once deciphered unveiled thousands of years of Egyptian history and the words of Ashoka deciphered by Prinsep that brought to light the greatness of that remarkable emperor from Ancient India.

Of all the museums in London, the British Museum was my favourite, and not just because it was so close to the place I was living in, on Malet Street. I visited it so often that it had been like home. Once you enter the museum, past the Grecian façade that faces Great Russell Street, the glass topped dome surrounding the cylindrical structure that was once the reading room of the British Library gives a unique sense of space, freedom and enlightenment that is hard to explain. Many a lazy afternoon had I spent there looking at the massive Ramses, looking down at me from across millennia, at the amazing stone sculptures of Ancient Greece, the copies of which I had seen in my school history books, and at the great bulls of Assyria. The benign smiling face of Buddha from Ancient China would face me one day and another day, I might come across the undeciphered history of the Easter Island statutes or African voodoo sculptures. As ancient worlds came alive I realized how small we are— our own lifetimes and our own worlds in the great march of time— and how those great kings and emperors would have felt immortal in their days, full of their immediate concerns, their momentary victories and fragile empires.

The Science Museum in South Kensington, London, impressed me with the spectacular heights reached by man's mind, but the Natural History Museum next door showed that man, with all his achievements and glories, was just a tiny speck in the story of Earth and that before us huge and powerful creatures had ruled this planet, only to vanish one day, to be preserved in fossils for kids to see later.

I wondered whether everybody around me felt the same. Perhaps not, and it was better that way as every artefact would reflect differently in the viewer's own history and frame of reference. And so the old grey-haired British lady would have perhaps viewed Tipu Sultan's dagger differently from me, and the Chinese youth would have had a different take on the exhibits on Ming Dynasty than the Tibetan monk.

I like to think that these differences and our acceptance of such inevitable differences, the acceptance of this 'otherness', is what progress of civilization is all about. How we look at 'others' and 'ourselves', how we come to terms with our differences and yet make common cause—have determined, and continue to determine, how life, civilization and history unfolds.

Such thoughts may appear to be profound and a tad pretentious, but I guess it was the fault of all those museums and galleries of London—profound, learned and a bit pretentious.

On the Shores of Lake Windermere

Generally, the Lake District and the Cornish Coast are considered to be the two most beautiful places in England, with the Yorkshire Dales competing. No doubt this is greatly aided and abetted by the considerable publicity literature generated by the tourism industry every day. I was quite sure that there would be equally beautiful natural vistas to startle the unsuspecting traveller in the valley of River Devon or on the sea coast of Norfolk, but still my feet and mind could not resist the temptation to visit Lake District, which was famous, quite deservedly too as I was to find out, as much for its natural beauty as for its romantic association with the great poet William Wordsworth.

However, it was a grey, cloudy and rainy Saturday morning when we boarded our northbound train from Euston Station in London. The station, one of the oldest in London and therefore in the world, used to have a historic, beautiful building before it was pulled down amidst some amount of public protest in the seventies. The only reminder of that today is the monumental arch that stands in front, with names of various destination stations engraved on its façade. Today's modern station building is no doubt spacious and efficiently functional, but to my mind it lacks that bit of character and history, especially in comparison to the majestic front of the nearby St Pancras Station.

Our train travelled north through the heart of England, with its gently sloping moist green hills, urban sprawls, small old villages with their church spires, steam-age railway stations with single platforms, grey brick façades and iron-and-steel roofs. There would only occasionally be something to startle the observant eye—a giant sculpture shaped like an open palm at Stoke-on-Trent Station or a huge steel arch dominating the skyscape over the famous Wembley Stadium. After a long journey, by English standards (a very short one by Indian standards), the train slowly eased into the station at Windermere that stood at the end of a branch line.

Nothing could be more different to the hustle and bustle of Euston Station than the terminating station at Windermere, with its solitary platform. Windermere is also the farthest one can travel by train into Lake District. Of course, officially or administratively, it was the county of Cumbria we had reached, with its headquarters at Carlisle, but it was Windermere, England's largest lake, and the number of other lakes surrounding it, that gave Lake District its popular name as well as its unique attraction and popularity.

As in so many parts of England, as elsewhere, the advent of the first steam-powered locomotive in the nineteenth century changed Windermere forever, and today it is difficult to even imagine what the little village of Windermere would have been like in the days of Wordsworth—a cluster of stone and wood huts, perhaps a solitary stone cottage of the landlord overlooking his lands, the lonely shores of the lake, a small village chapel and perhaps a public house. Although today it is difficult to distinguish between the two, the village on the shores of the lake is called Bowness and is separate from the village of Windermere, which is some two miles up the lake road that is spread around the railway station.

Our quaint little hotel, delightfully close to a swift mountain brook, was situated near the boundary of the two villages and was therefore perfectly distant from the touristy hustle and bustle that dominated the lake shore. I was once again reminded of the fact that, India could never be too far away while travelling in Britain, as our landlady had been born in Breech Candy Hospital in what was then called Bombay! Her parents and her grandparents had spent their working lives in colonial India. She had herself spent her childhood in then Bangalore and in Ooty, which she called 'Ooctamund'.

Coming to Windermere, I was instantly transported to the mall of Ranikhet and the 'Thandi Sadak' of Nainital, and although there were significant differences—in terms of population, in civic amenities and levels of pollution—the similarities were striking. Here, one begins to understand that what must have inspired the Englishmen, or rather the British, to make their cottages in the hill stations of India—in Ranikhet, Nainital, Mussoorie, Simla, Darjeeling and Ooty. Looking out of the windows of my cosy little room, I could imagine being somewhere in the outskirts of a hill stations in India, perhaps somewhere between Ranikhet and Chaubattia or perhaps between Mussoorie and the Everest Bungalow.

Cruising on Lake Windermere is considered to be one of those must-do activities on a visit to Lake District, as is a visit to the museum dedicated to Beatrix Potter, a famous writer of children's stories, who is perhaps more famous today in England than elsewhere. But a short but delightful steam train journey from Lakeside—through the green forests, along the swiftly flowing blue waters of a mountain stream, over Newby Bridge—was much more enjoyable. The train journey—in carefully restored ancient wooden carriages, with the breeze wafting through the open windows and steam suspended thickly in the air—through small, delightful, single platform railway stations with ancient steel girder footbridges will remain etched in my memory.

There was still broad daylight, even at seven in the evening, by the time we returned to the shores of the lake, and although the cruises had stopped operating for the day, whole families, many of them from South Asia, were still enjoying the day in the grassy Glen Park that overlooked the lake. Once again, as elsewhere in Britain, I was reminded of how Indians, Pakistanis, Bangladeshis, and even Sri Lankans and Nepalis, seemed virtually to be one people and how difficult it was for them to meet and know each other in the subcontinent itself.

Although there are Indian restaurants everywhere in Britain, catering to both Indians and Englishmen, that are doing rather well, their food, with honourable exceptions, is mostly indifferent and sometimes horrible to the Indian palate. It is better, even if one is vegetarian, or vegan, to go for something local at someplace patronized by the locals. Hotel Beresford at Windermere has seen better days, but its old grey-haired steward and its continental and English dishes were authentic and friendly, qualities that are not so apparent in more touristy places.

One of the chief attractions in Windermere is the beautifully marked footpaths, which go through green farms and lovely woods, with perhaps a solitary mountain brook accompanying one along for some part of the way. Some times a wild hare would suddenly cross one's path; sometimes a beautiful glimpse of the still and shining water of the lake would offer itself at some quiet turn.

The weather was especially nice and sunny the day after our arrival, and I took a walk in the morning on the so-called 'Sheriff's Walk' through the woods to the lake shore. It reminded me of another time and place—of the numerous walks that I had taken back in India years ago as a young man, in the hills of what is today the state of Uttarakhand. It was another place, another time, perhaps it was another me, but the scent of mountain air, the sound of birds chirping and flowing water from an invisible brook, the play of sunlight through the branches of the Deodar-like English cedar trees— all appeared to be somewhat familiar. It is on such walks in the deep solitude of nature, away from the maddening crowds of tourists, that one realizes why, for years, these places in Lake District have attracted people from all over England and beyond, not only to visit but also to build their homes and settle down.

And it was on these very shores of Lake Windermere that some three hundred children had been provided with their first homes after their terrible ordeal in Nazi concentration camps, just after the end of World War II. To most of them, it felt like heaven, as I was informed during a beautifully evocative exhibition that was being held during our stay. It was called, quite poignantly, 'From Auschwitz to Ambleside' and was being shown in the historic library building of Windermere, situated amidst beautiful flowering trees in a splendid garden. Today, it is difficult to even imagine what must have gone through the minds of those children—relief at having escaped almost certain death, terrible sorrow and grief of knowing the loss of near and dear ones, uncertainty about their future in a foreign and unknown land? But it was inspiring to know that, despite everything, most of them grew up to be not only content and useful citizens of society but also living reminders for the world of their terrible experiences and of what the world should not allow ever again. I hoped that their efforts had not been in vain.

In the evening I stopped over at a local grocery-cum-souvenir shop to buy some famous Kendal mint cake. The cake, which gets its name from the nearby town of Kendal, is nice, sweet and nourishing but is not really a cake; it is a type of mint candy and has been used for its reportedly energizing qualities by athletes and adventurers. Just like an English muffin is not really a muffin and a Yorkshire pudding is not really a pudding, I learnt, the Kendal mint cake is not at all a cake. I thought the Kendal mint cake would be the most appropriate and befitting snack to accompany the first British Mount Everest summiteer.

As I rummaged through the grocery store, waiting my turn, the headlines of the various newspapers of the day showed that, for the first time in more than a hundred years, party other than a Conservative and Labour had polled more votes in the recently concluded European Union (EU) elections. It was widely believed that the far right United Kingdom Independent Party (UKIP) had benefitted from its anti-immigration and anti-EU stands. Was Britain changing and closing its mind to the outside world, I wondered. It was difficult to know, especially for a traveller, and only time would answer such questions for sure, but it appeared to me that, despite what people and political parties wanted, it was too late for the country to change and that sheer 'path dependence' would determine the country's future.

That night I slept off listening to the news of UKIP's victory but not before enjoying some good old Hindi film songs of my early childhood that were being broadcast from BBC's Asia TV network. I wondered whether this too was going to change. Who knows? That was, as I remember, my very last thought that last night at Windermere, as the gentle sound of a mountain brook lulled me to sleep.

The Branch Line to St Ives

Even in my early childhood I always loved train journeys. I especially remember the anticipation with which I awaited them when *we*, as a family, used to board the Rajdhani Express for the long journey to Calcutta. That love for train journeys has persisted, and though England, because of its modest size, did not offer the opportunity for such long journeys as in India, I would try, during my stay in London, to take whatever opportunities that came my way to make a train journey.

One of the longest of those was also one of the quickest when I undertook a train journey from London to the almost extreme west of England, to a tiny but beautiful town on the coast of Celtic Sea called St Ives. We boarded the train from Paddington Station in London, a station whose name always evoked images of Sherlock Holmes and Dr Watson, racing through the crowded, smoke-filled, noisy platforms more than a century ago. The station, although modernized in a conformist sort of way, still retains some of its original character and atmosphere. Soon we were off to the west of

England, familiar to me only from the pages of English novels from my childhood. The landscape outside was pretty in an unspectacular sort of way—the rolling green fields interrupted by small towns and villages, an occasional canal or a church spire.

Although St Ives is a rather touristy destination, we were travelling in the so-called 'off season', and so the train was conveniently empty, and the few passengers, other than us, in our carriage appeared to be all locals, travelling from one intermediate station to another—from home to work, to family, to the market. The only exceptions were three old British women, apparently happily retired, who were out to enjoy a holiday on their own and who were volubly amazed at almost every turn of scene outside. Their zest and innocence was contagious. Maybe they had, for the first time, disentangled themselves from their burdensome obligations to live their own lives.

There is something about a train journey that makes me, not exactly hungry, want to eat or munch. It was always so. As a child I used to eagerly wait for the time when hot rice, chapattis, chicken curry and curd were served in the Rajdhani Express. In the days gone by, passengers would leisurely have meals at the railway station restaurants while the train waited on the platform. But now, even the practice of well-appointed dining cars is slowly giving way, at least in England where privatization of the railways has gone hand-in-hand with considerations of cost minimization and profit maximization. The passenger is left to content himself with a stroll down the corridors to a vendor of cold sandwiches and crisps in one of the carriages. The vendor in that train that day was one Mr Hamid, as I read from his nameplate. He claimed, on being asked, that he belonged to Rawalpindi in Pakistan. Although it is not so uncommon to hear Urdu in London of today, still to hear a familiar tongue in a foreign land is always heartening, and I told him as much.

The real beauty of the train journey to St Ives was in the short branch line that took us from St Erth to St Ives. This train line, which has somehow managed to escape scrapping in England's quest for economization and efficiency, is a throwback to a period when life was more relaxed and people had more time to stop and stare. The relaxed speed and tiny size of the train, the small, deserted stations on the way, the courtesy of the attendant, and most of all the spectacular beauty of the ocean with its foaming waves sparking in the last light of day, as the train snaked through the coastal cliffs, made this short journey one of the most memorable. Much more than a century ago, this beautiful branch line to St Ives was laid down by Victorian engineers and crewmen in the golden age of railways, and it will indeed be a shame if/when it falls under the merciless hammer of the economizing politician.

By the time the train reached the pretty little station of St Ives darkness had descended. Through the slight drizzle I could see the short glistening arrows of raindrops against the bright lights of the deserted station. From prior knowledge, courtesy: Google, I knew that the sea lay straight ahead of me, across the dark abyss, but it was the sound of the waves and the red, blinking light of a distant lighthouse that gave away its presence. The bay of St Ives lay below us, to our left, inviting us with its glittering lights, spread across a gently sloping, low hill.

I was looking forward to my stay in St Ives and, pretty as it was reputed to be, to travel around in the countryside made famous by Virginia Woolf and Thomas Hardy, but at that moment, on that evening, as the train made its way back to St Erth, leaving the station of St Ives completely deserted but for us, I longed for the transient warmth and certainty that only a slowly moving train carriage could bring to the soul of a traveller.

The Churches in London

Without considering the controversy created by former British Prime Minister David Cameron's statement regarding Britain being a Christian country, it is safe to admit that the Christian Church has exerted enormous influence not only in Britain but also in entire Europe, over almost all aspects of European civilization. Western classical music owes its origin, in significant measure, to the music of church choirs; the arts can trace their origins to the medieval altar paintings and the paintings made on the walls and roofs of churches. The architecture, literature, social customs, practices and sanctions, politics and even warfare, as seen most dramatically in the Crusades, have been enormously affected by the Christian church. This is not to negate the pre-Christian or other influences on European civilization, but rather to acknowledge the fact that the church has been one of the principal influences on the lives, and even deaths, of the people of Europe.

So it was a bit surprising, to me at least, to read somewhere that almost a quarter of the British population today had, in the most recent census, declared that they had had no religion. What did this imply? Was it a fashion? A desire for individualism? A rebellion against the establishment, conventional mores and institutions? Materialism? All of those? None of the above? I can't say, but I suspect that even for those people who like to profess atheism—the church and its tradition affect them in many conscious and unconscious ways.

The churches in London, and there are many in central London itself, invariably belong to a different era, and their present, impressive buildings, mostly English Gothic, are from centuries ago. Most of them follow the Church of England that owes its origin to King Henry VIII's quarrel with the then pope, avowedly over issues pertaining to his marriages rather than over theological problem. Undoubtedly, the two most impressive and famous of them are Westminster Abbey and St Paul's Cathedral, and invariably one encounters hordes of tourists from all over the world, with their backpacks and cameras, moving around and inside these two most famous of London's churches. The Westminster Abbey, situated right next to the Parliament, is more of a royal church where historically all coronations took place—another symbol of Britain indeed being a Christian country. St Paul's, on the other hand, situated in the heart of the city, is considered more of a people's church, although the ill-fated royal wedding of the Prince of Wales and Lady Diana Spencer took place here.

Westminster Abbey is near English Gothic, and has spawned numerous clones not only all over Britain but also wherever the British went and settled around the world. On the other hand, St Paul's, or more correctly the present building of St Paul's, a creation of Sir Christopher Wren that has stood for more than three centuries now, is quite different from the usual English church. It has that spectacular and beautiful dome that has remained an enduring symbol of London's skyline, even when much taller buildings—the latest being the skyscraper called 'The Shard'—have been allowed to come up. The image of the silhouette of St Paul's dome against a dark and bleak London sky during the days of the German Blitz in World War II is one of the iconic images of the resilience of the British in their 'finest hour'.

Much has been written about St Paul's and its architecture, from the harmonious proportions of its massive lead-clad dome to its 'whispering galleries', which run along the base of the dome and offer special views of the spectacularly painted roof, to the mosaic that adorns its walls and of the various chapels inside. But for many a tourist, the most remarkable feature of a visit to St Paul's is the spectacular views of London to be had upon climbing up the narrow staircases to reach the top of the dome. St Paul's height and location ensure that one sees, especially on a sunny and clear day, one of the most spectacular views of London—the Tower Bridge spanning the River Thames, the various boats and vessels moving or marooned over the gleaming surface of 'the Pool', people walking along the two embankments on either side of the River, the spires and bell towers of the various 'lesser' churches of London, the gleaming modern office towers of the city. It is a view that manages to encapsulate London in one three-sixty degree panorama as nothing else does.

As I had noticed time and again in Britain, India could never be far away. And so too in the various memorials and epitaphs in St Paul's, there were numerous reminders of India—the life-size statue of famous Indologist William Jones holding a carved stone copy of the Manusmriti; the memorial to Sir Henry Lawrence, the doomed last chief commissioner of Awadh who died in 1857 in the 'defence of Lucknow'; or the celebrated memorial to the Duke of Wellington, whose formative years were spent in the battlefields of India, fighting against the Marathas and Tipu. I was reminded once again of how much the English history of the last three centuries is inextricably and, many a time, unfortunately linked with that of the vast subcontinent. Much has been written about the effects of the British Empire on India, much less on the effect of India on the British—on their culture, language, cuisine, but most importantly on their collective mind space and how it has transformed their view of the world and their view of themselves, their view of the past, present and future.

Apart from these two obvious stalwarts of London churches, there are many others, some of them centuries old. The Anglican church of St Martin-in-the-fields, situated right next to Trafalgar Square, points to a distant past when the surrounding areas of rushing traffic were nothing but farmlands. I had enjoyed many a silent afternoon under its high ceilings, in spacious solitude, with sunlight peering in through its stained glass windows, away from the rush and restless energy of the surrounding megacity.

I also remember enjoying a lovely violin concert in the cavernous interiors of the 'new' St Pancras Church, on one Friday afternoon, by a young woman of Indian descent, under the proud and watchful eyes of her parents. I remember I had attended Midnight Mass on Christmas Eve in a church on Regent Street, more out of respectful curiosity than from any fervent religious belief. The modernistic sermon was couched in idioms and phrases of the twenty-first century, and the ancient hymns were led by a person, who as his surname went, had belonged to the Indian subcontinent. It was a beautiful service, and the feelings and thoughts expressed were very similar in substance to the underlying themes of my own religion and inherited traditions, formed by a curious and complex amalgamation of Western influence and Indian thought and mores. As I looked around me, I realized that the ancient voice of a shepherd saint was speaking from across centuries, centuries when the church that functioned in his name had sometimes made people suffer, had sometimes led them to violence, but the eternal message of piety and love was still strong enough to move the people who had assembled in the church that night. The essential unity of humanity was so clearly revealed in that congregation on Christmas Eve, and I was glad that I had decided, almost as an afterthought, to venture out that cold night.

Across the 'Border' to Scotland

One of the most remarkable things about Scotland in general, and Edinburgh in particular, is the high esteem in which the Scotsman holds the thinkers, writers and philosophers of his land. There are a remarkable number of memorials dedicated to them, and these adorn the most prominent parts of the city. As my train gently floated into the old and impressive railway station of Edinburgh Waverley, the most famous and most iconic of these memorials, a tall, dark, spire-like monument dedicated to Sir Walter Scott, loomed in front of my eager eyes. It was only much later that the fact registered in my mind that 'Waverly' was the name of one of Scott's most famous novels, and I was reminded of how long ago I had come across one of his other novels, *Ivanhoe*, in a long-forgotten corner of a bookshelf in my father's attic in Kolkata.

Like most of the old and famous cities of Europe—although the modern city has spread in many directions for miles—the historic city of Edinburgh is situated in a rather small area, from the castle on one side to the Palace of

Holyroodhouse on other. It was the last week of May, and the sun was refusing to set. The fine balmy weather and the clear blue sky, on that first of my evenings in Scotland, prompted me to explore the city, although it was rather late in the day. And so I left my guest house that was run by an immigrant family from Iraq, of all places, to explore the heart if not the soul of Edinburgh. And I decided to do so on foot. To walk through the centre of a historic town in Europe on a sunny summer afternoon, without any cares on your mind, is one of the greatest pleasures.

Groups of tourists were moving towards Edinburgh Castle that loomed over the grey–black hill dominating the skyline of the city for miles. The formidable ramparts, the moat, the drawbridge, the gates and towers and, most of all, the prison cells indicated towards time in history when peace and stability couldn't be taken for granted and when wars, violent rebellions and equally violent repressions and class exploitation were the order of the day.

From the castle, the famous Royal Mile stretched straight, through the heart of the historic city centre up to the Palace of Holyroodhouse. The Palace, now the home of the queen whenever she is in Edinburgh, has a tumultuous and poignant history that stretches back to the times when Scotland had its own monarchy. Today, it may be difficult for an outsider to imagine that Scotland once had its own king and queen, its own state and government and that the Scots fought for and protected their independence for centuries against the English.

At the time of my visit, Scotland was to decide in three months' time—this time through ballot boxes rather than on the battleground—whether they wanted to live with England or not. I could see signature campaigns and polite canvassing going on in street corners in favour of an independence vote, but in my many conversations with the Scots, whom I met during the visit, the population seemed to have no overwhelming opinion either way, and there seemed to be a lot of doubt and uncertainty about the future. Perhaps it was these same feelings of insecurity that averted the breakaway of Scotland three months later.

Just like the Buckingham Palace in London, the Palace of Holyroodhouse, where Queen Elizabeth II lives when she is in Edinburgh, is situated in the heart of the city with no protective bastions or security rings around it. The contrast between the Palace on one end of the Royal Mile and Edinburgh Castle on the other is quite stark, that way. The Palace, just like the Castle, is a reflection of its times, when the security of the monarch resided in the will and acceptance of the people rather than on the strength of his/her troops. Today democracy rules, and as a result the Scottish Parliament building, ironically stands directly opposite the Palace of Holyroodhouse.

The present Scottish Parliament came to life again, after a hiatus of centuries, at the turn of the millennium. I remember having watched the telecast of the opening session of the Scottish Parliament in 1999, an event that was understandably full of emotions and feelings, wherein a lady parliamentarian—I forget the name—had chosen to recite the immortal lines of Robert Burn's 'A man is a man and all that'. The fact that a nation which can boast of world-famous writers like Sir Walter Scott and R.L. Stevenson, of Dr Jekyll and Mr

Hyde fame, decided to name Robert Burns as its national poet is indicative of not only the enduring greatness of his verses but also the inspiring touch of his poetry on Scottish nationhood, often latent, over the centuries. That evening, as I stood opposite the Scottish Parliament building with my back to the Palace of Holyroodhouse, two opposing streams of history, of the people's voice, emerging through centuries of hierarchy and authority, appeared to come to life against the beautiful sunset over the clear blue sky of Edinburgh.

From the days of Fergusson and Burns, the writings of Alexander McCall Smith, to the days of J.K. Rowling and her creation Harry Potter—Edinburgh has moved on. Edinburgh was said to have been created in a café on George IV Bridge, appropriately called the 'Elephant Café', as it is decorated with hundreds of statues and replicas of elephants. Edinburgh has emerged as a major tourist destination, and I could see, among others, a number of families from the Indian subcontinent— young, professional, double income parents with their babies in perambulators; joint families in which the young earning generation had taken its old parents for their first vacation abroad; students studying at the famed Edinburgh University, where once Acharya Prafulla Chandra Ray had studied; and even resident families going about their daily chores—the office-home-Tesco routine.

Edinburgh has more than its share of usual touristy attractions: Edinburgh Castle, Palace of Holyroodhouse, a royal yacht tethered at the port, galleries and museums, memorials, shopping districts and touristy avenues. But I particularly loved visiting a not-so-famous, small museum called 'The Writer's Museum', which was beautifully and lovingly curated inside a medieval three-storeyed building in the heart of the city. It was easy to miss the engravings on the pavement stones in the courtyard—of famous sentences written by many famous Scottish writers of yore. Inside the Museum, Robert Burns, Sir Walter Scott and R.L. Stevenson occupied, deservedly, pride of place, and not only their lives and writings but also the Scotland of their time—the society and people—were brought to life through the exhibits. The statues of kings and dukes of bygone times still loom in the dark street corners of Edinburgh, where nobody stops. Today these important men of their times are almost forgotten, but the words of the men of minds and letters, and of others like Adam Smith, whose imposing statue stands at the heart of the Royal Mile, continue to inspire generations all over the world. So Burn's 'Auld Lang Syne' continues to enthral innumerable New Year's Eve celebrations and passing-out parades all over the world, and *Ivanhoe* is still read by youth, thousands of miles away.

As the evening turned grey and dark, a slight drizzle brought the temperature down. It was summer, but I could imagine how dark and cold Edinburgh must have been in its long winter months before the advent of electricity, street lights and central heating, how ruthless the climate and, consequently, how meagre the cultivation would have been in those days. I could understand why whiskey became the iconic drink of this land, why warm, woven kilts became their favoured dress and why meat, potatoes and turnip became the principal ingredients of their unchristened national dish, haggis and tatties.

The human being has lived and adapted himself to all sorts of habitats and climates, and still man has never been content to merely survive. His mind has sought to go beyond mere survival or enjoyment, and has risen up and has even dared to touch the Divine itself. In my mind, it is these heights of human thought, rather than the height of the towers of the Palace or that of the ramparts of the Edinburgh Castle, that make Edinburgh such a special city.

PART 2
Criss-crossing the Continent

All Roads Lead to Rome

Six years ago, to the day that I write this, I visited Rome for the first time. I remember this especially because it was Poila Boishakh then, the Bengali New Year. Then, I accidentally came across a celebration by local Bangladeshi residents of Rome, as I have mentioned in *A Passage across Europe*.[3] The memory was the very first thought that crossed my mind as my train eased into Rome's Termini Station, as it had done six years ago. The station looked the same, but then the interiors of all large railway stations, anywhere in the modern world looked similar, from King's Cross in London to Gare du Nord in Paris, to the Termini in Rome.

I was not particularly keen to *do* the usual tourist circuit. I had fancied myself as a traveller soaking up the sights, sounds and smells of a place. But like all tourists, I really couldn't afford to spend the time—days and weeks—required to get

---

[3] Sen Sharma, P. (2012), *A Passage Across Europe*, IInd Edn., Sahitya Bhandar: Allahabad.

under the skin of a place. I was afraid that in my effort I would miss everything without gaining anything. So the next morning, I found myself standing in front of the Coliseum, the eternal symbol of Rome's ancient splendour and glory. It was a lovely day, with clear blue sunny skies, and it was thankfully a bit early for the usual crowd of tourist, and the Coliseum was not crowded. More than half of its impressive façade was covered with scaffolding, indicating the massive restoration work that was taking place. It struck me that what stood in front of me was the first-ever stadium, the first-ever arena, the first-ever Wembley or Eden Gardens. Today, it is difficult to imagine crowds, two thousand years ago, baying for blood, while the proud emperors watched and the valiant and yet helpless gladiators fought against hungry wild animals. Memories of numerous Hollywood movies—*The Gladiator*, *Spartacus*, *Ben Hur*—forced themselves into my mind, maybe aided by the kitsch Roman soldiers that had started appearing around me, luring tourists to take photographs with them.

Soon I retraced my own steps of six years ago, through the Imperia de Flori, the street that runs through the very heart of ancient Rome. I realized that I had been retracing not only my own steps but also the steps of Julius Caesar, of Cicero, of perhaps Michelangelo and definitely Mussolini; I had walked down a street covered with the dust of history. The massive ruins of the Imperial Fora lay in front of me, spread out like an open museum, as I stood on top of a low hill, with the replica statue of the original 'philosopher king', Emperor Marcus Aurelius, behind me. The square where I stood was impressive, because of both its location and the façades of the palaces (now museums) that surrounded it. However, I couldn't find anything special about the Michelangelo-designed stairs that lead up to the square. Curiously, the bronze statue of Marcus Aurelius stood with its back to the Imperial Fora and the Coliseum, as if in a deliberate stance to distance himself from the gory glory and violent splendour of ancient Rome. The thoughts and 'meditations' of this rather reluctant emperor, a man chosen for his abilities and not by any accident of birth, have travelled across centuries and have inspired generations of men searching for the elusive answers to life's eternal questions.

For a city with over two-and-a-half millennia of uninterrupted history, six years was just a blink of an eye, and yet I was trying to detect how the eternal city had changed since my last visit. The Pantheon was exactly the same as I had remembered, with its massive dome, oculus, Raphael's tomb, its slightly sloping floors of coloured marble and its much later additions of marble statues of Christian saints, occupying the same niches that once had pre-Christian deities, and, of course, the crowds of tourists clicking away, following the multilingual guides. Although originally built for other deities, the Pantheon remains the oldest church building in the world, something that is generally lost to the majority of viewers as it, naturally, does not look like what we expect a church to be like. Nevertheless, uniformed and officious men were busy silencing the chattering tourists, trying to remind them that, indeed, even today the Pantheon remains a place of worship and not merely a touristic curiosity.

In Rome, as one walks a yard one finds oneself traversing centuries. So within a few yards, I moved from the pre-Christian era, when the Pantheon had been used as a place of worship, to the Renaissance period when Trevi Fountain, its huge marble façade curiously adorned with pre-Christian pantheistic gods, had been built under the orders of medieval popes. I remembered I had thrown a coin into the fountain during my last visit to honour the superstition that it would bring me back to Rome someday. And here I was, once again standing in front of Trevi Fountain.

Rome remained a fascinating city, but something stopped me this time from throwing another coin into the fountain. Maybe it was my age; maybe it was my desire to return home, maybe it was the noisy crowd all around me maybe it was my desire to challenge accepted wisdom; maybe all of these.

But Rome is very much a living city, and although today it may not be the centre of the Western world, as it used to be in the days when people in the Imperial Fora had ruled over an area that extended from Ephesus (in today's Turkey) to the city of York in northern England, to Volubilis in Morocco, Rome still attracts tourists, travellers, businessmen, artists, immigrants and charlatans from all over the world. One such immigrant was playing an accordion in front of me as I sat in one of the numerous pavement cafés of Piazza Navona. Suddenly my unsuspecting ears could detect the familiar tune of an age-old, long-forgotten Hindi film song, '*Chahe koi khush ho chahe galiayan hazar de*'. Obviously, there was some common origin somewhere, embedded in some forgotten misty moment of antiquity, when this piece of music had been created somewhere in the mind and fingers of some artist and had since then travelled over years and miles in ways unimaginable to the original creator. It is such unexpected moments that suddenly make travelling interesting, and one realizes how the numerous invisible hands of history are shaping every moment of our present, our future.

Paulo was a typical modern day 'Roman', as he liked to call himself, and a proud one at that. He took the impressive heritage of his city as something given and was more concerned about the weekend's football match between his club and S.S. Lazio, as we sat on his terrace, overlooking a beautiful crimson-blue sunset over one of the hills that make up Rome. He loved spicy, Indian food as he loved his own cuisine, and in-between incessant cigarettes and somewhat abrupt English, we groped around for common topics of conversation: ancient Rome, modern Italian politics, Indian elections, the upcoming football world cup and his childhood memories. His partner, Laura, was from Belfast but had lived in India for some years and had travelled through cities of my childhood and youth—Delhi, Varanasi and Agra. She knew a lot about India, far more than I had expected. Unfortunately, I barely knew anything about Northern Ireland to reciprocate her knowledge and her curiosity about my country. Somehow the only impressions about Northern Ireland I had, or still have, were of wet, dripping streets, dark pubs, good whisky, sea and a beautiful countryside.

Such chance acquaintances, accidental conversations, beautiful sunsets over terraces, pieces of unexpected yet familiar music, along with the usual touristy 'done' things of monuments and sights recommended by tourist guidebooks, made up my trip to Rome. I didn't throw a coin into Trevi Fountain this time, so I would have to wait to find out whether my road, someday, again would lead to the eternal city.

Along Lake Geneva

For the statesmen, diplomats and bureaucrats who congregate in the Swiss city of Geneva, to attend the many conferences hosted by international organizations, the Lake would probably merely mean an occasional walk along the manicured promenade, looking at the Jetd' Eau or 'water jet'— the fountain on Lake Geneva—or at the Flower Clock, or taking an evening stroll on the Mont Blanc Bridge that connects the two sides of the city. But Lake Geneva is immense. I think many more than a hundred Nainitals can get subsumed in it. But apart from its size, the dramatic backdrop of the snow-capped Alps overlooking it makes it one of the most beautiful lakes anywhere in the world.

I was fortunate to have been driven by Joan, a friend, to the tiny village of Yvoir on the French side of the lake, far from the madding crowd, as without her I would never have been able to look at the serene beauty of the lake from such a peaceful setting. It was a lazy, sunny, Tuesday, and the streets of the village, a declared Heritage Site, were devoid of the usual hordes of camera-wielding tourists. We walked slowly under the ruins of the medieval gates of the village to the small harbour. Today the village was an example of those diversions of the rich when they wanted to playact 'close to nature' with all modern amenities available, and one could find sleek BMWs and Ferraris parked in front of carefully maintained, medieval-looking houses, in which once poor farmers had lived. Expensive boats and yachts stood in the harbour alongside the few remaining fishing boats of the original residents. As I stood gazing at the still blue–grey waters of the lake that shimmered in the sunlight, as if jewels had been carelessly spread on its surface, an old man with a flowing white beard on a dilapidated motorboat—a veritable Hemingway-esque 'old man'—floated into the harbour. Suddenly the silence of the moment was shattered as the bells of the village church (with a stainless steel-plated, onion-shaped dome) rang out across the tiny ripples of the surface of the lake.

Not so long ago, the now almost deserted church and its priest would have dominated the social, economic and religious lives of the simple, God-fearing villagers, who would have been completely dependent on the harvest of their fishing boats, on their sheep that grazed on the grassy hills and on the bit of seasonal farming. There would have been neither the possibility nor the need of any contact with the outside world, and a man, and especially a woman, would have been content to live and die in the village, without once venturing beyond its boundaries. Although the walls and the houses had been artificially maintained to resemble the bygone era, in an attempt to evoke selective nostalgia, it was difficult for me to delude myself. I couldn't overlook the stark modern jets flying overhead or the Korean tourist girl who had just then entered the harbour with her French boyfriend. This attempt of Europeans to cling on to an imagined beauty of peaceful medieval times perhaps provided them with an illusory sense of satisfaction. For the same age had also epic epidemics, severe class oppression by the aristocracy and church, gross violence and grinding drudgery, freezing houses and dark nights. But then man had been blessed with selective memory, and I thanked God for that.

The next day, I took a train ride from Geneva Railway Station to Montreux, using the Swiss pass that I had the good sense to purchase before entering Switzerland. On the Swiss side of the lake, unlike the French side, an excellent railway line runs all along the banks of the lake, and apart from the city of Geneva itself, other smaller but equally beautiful cities like Lausanne, Nyon and Montreux lie along the edge. The train offers the traveller dramatic landscapes of towering snow-clad Alpine peaks, above the clear still blue–grey waters of the lake, but the people commuting everyday on these trains seemed immune to such unearthly beauty. True, I had seen even taller and more majestic Himalayan peaks in India, but to get to look at them from close quarters—one had to travel for days on foot, and here I was sitting comfortably in my railway carriage and looking at a clear hundred-and-eighty degree vista of jaw-dropping beauty; snow-covered mountains reflected on the largest Alpine lake in Europe, as the train skimmed along its banks.

Joan had returned to her hometown of Lyon the same morning, and I was truly grateful to her for all her time and patience with this vagabond, but at that moment I was secretly glad to travel alone too since such beauty in front of my eyes demanded total silence and solitude.

An Evening in Graz, Austria

For most of us Indians, Vienna is the only city that comes to mind when we think of Austria. The few who have had the good fortune to have travelled around a bit may know of Salzburg, of *The Sound of Music* fame, and may even know of Innsbruck, the headquarters of the famed Swarovski Crystals. But Graz, the second largest city in Austria, is relatively unknown to Indians, although its city centre has been named as a UNESCO Heritage Site for now almost ten years. So I considered myself doubly fortunate for the opportunity to visit Graz, even if only for one evening, that summer.

It took us around three hours on the highway to reach Graz from the Vienna Airport, having reached the latter on our Air India 6034 flight from New Delhi. We were staying in a century-old hotel called Das Weitzman situated on the banks of the River Mur. The hotel was excellently located and was quite near to the historic city centre but not right in it. Unlike many other rivers of Europe, I found River Mur to be fast-flowing, and its currents, strengthened by the recent rain showers, reminded me of our own Himalayan mountain rivers, such as the Bhagirathi and Alaknanda, with their volatile beauty, although the surroundings were spectacularly different.

Like many other European cities, such as Budapest and Ljubljana, in Graz too a river, Mur—divides the city into two parts, distinct from each other not only in geography and topography but also in history and architecture. The opposite bank of River Mur is relatively flat topographically and relatively new. This difference between the two banks of the river is mainly due to the fact that the science and craft of building bridges is of comparatively recent origin; and hence the river used to act as a natural frontier for the old city in the old days.

By the time I had finished my work and work-related engagements, it was nearly four in the afternoon, but it was springtime in Europe, and I knew that sunlight would remain till around nine. I had some time to stroll through and explore the city of Graz on my own. It was drizzling; and therefore, armed with a borrowed umbrella and a road map, I started on my solitary excursion into the heart of Graz.

After a kilometre or so of working along River Mur, I found a prominent building that stood out, starkly different from the other surrounding buildings. This was the modern museum house—a huge, black, glass Kunthouse surfaced, submarine-like structure with truncated antenna-like vents to let in light through the roof. It was designed by a famous British architect and was hardly a decade old and showed that the citizens were not content to live off the city's rich history alone but were keen to add to its legacy in their own lifetime.

Further up the river bank was another marvellous and recent architectural addition to the city's landscape—Murinsel, a glass-domed, artificial island in the midst of the fast-flowing river, connected to the two banks and supported by two pedestrian bridges. There was a café in the glass-domed island, but it appeared to be totally deserted that evening when I crossed over the river, through the Murinsel, to the other older and richer bank of the river.

Almost directly in front of me, rising gently was the green hill called the Schlossberg, which had been the centre of the lives of the citizens of Graz throughout centuries. I could see the old clock tower, with its grey–black roof, somewhere half up on the hillside, which the locals called 'Urhturm' in German.[4] Despite the drizzle, enthusiastic locals had been climbing up the hill on staircases cut on its side, some even with bicycles on their shoulders. For others less fanatical about fitness, there was a century-old but impeccably maintained, funicular railway called the Schlossbergbahn, which would move up the hill to the very top, almost at an angle of forty-five degrees, and had been doing so since 1905, although the carriages had been modernized and been made more comfortable, over the years.

However, before taking a ride up Schlossberg Hill, I decided to take a walk through the city centre, having already

---

[4] It is said by the locals that the Castle of Graz was never 'taken'; nevertheless during, Napoleonic attack on Austria, the castle walls were destroyed, and almost the only remnant of the old castle now is the clock tower called 'Urhturm', which the citizens of Graz could save from the hands of the French aggressors by paying a handsome ransom, and since then it has become the virtual symbol of the city itself.

decided to have a laid-back dinner later in the evening, at one of the restaurants located at the top of Schlossberg Hill. As I turned right from the ticket counters of Schlossbergbahn and walked through one of the cobblestone streets amidst silent trams, which seemed to be the principal mode of public transport in the city, I realized how *we*, in India, had all but discarded trams as an option of urban public transport amidst the growing clamour for metros, bus rapid transit systems (BRTS), monorails etc. Many continental European cities not only preserve and loved their trams but modernized them too.

The city centre was dominated by the impressive and huge façade of the town hall—'Rathaus', as they say in German, but to me the medieval legislative building nearby, Landhaus, was even more impressive. A local wine-tasting festival was being held in the courtyard inside. Wine producers from all across the Styrian region had assembled with the very best of their produce, and some of them were even dressed in medieval Styrian costumes, much to the enjoyment of the tourists.

I set off from Landhaus to keep my 6.00 p.m. appointment with the 'glockenspiel' clock, famous for its handcrafted, almost life-size statues—one of a man holding a jar of wine in his hand and another that of a woman—which come out at 6.00 p.m., revolving to the accompaniment of music. Before I could reach it, one helpful, old local citizen, who, having realized that I had been a solitary tourist, very kindly pointed me to a small house, where the famous physicist, astronomer and mathematician Johannes Kepler had lived a few centuries ago while he had been teaching mathematics at the University of Graz. The University still thrives, after more than three centuries. The sound of the church bells coming from the nearby Church of St Francis was a reminder of the Catholicism of the city. In the medieval period, during Kepler's time, the city was religiously intolerant, as was usual in those days, and it drove Kepler, a Lutheran, to leave Graz and emigrate permanently to Prague, where he lived and did most of his work and came up with his famous laws, which *we* grew up studying in our high school physics textbooks.

I reached my destination, the building that housed the glockenspiel clock, and at precisely 6.00 p.m., as they had day after day for centuries, a pair of windows at the top of the building opened up, and two handcrafted, almost life-size statues—one of a man holding a jar of wine in his hand and another that of a woman—came out, revolving around each other to the accompaniment of music. They have been acting as both time-keeper and a source of entertainment for the citizens of Graz for centuries.

A small group of locals and tourists had gathered in front of the three-storeyed building. The façade of the building was effusively painted, and it used to be a wine shop and a medieval drinking house, whose enterprising owner had got the glockenspiel clock installed, having first imported it from the Netherlands, thus adding yet another attraction to the city of Graz. Such clocks were not uncommon in Europe, and I had already seen one in Prague and another in Munich, but I had always found them to be part of a public building—a town hall or a church, for example. But in Graz, it was a result of a purely private enterprise and that too of a wine merchant.

It had been almost 8.00 p.m. by the time I began walking back along the river to Schlossbergbahn and took a ride up to the hilltop in the funicular. At the hilltop, there were appeared to be were what remains of the walls of the ancient castle that

Napoleon's forces destroyed and where today stood a number of posh restaurants, overlooking the city below.

It was time to take a window seat and have a relaxed dinner of local, white Styrian wine and local cuisine Wiener schnitzel with potato fries, while of at the city below slowly come to light against the backdrop of the blue–grey sky and the distant horizon. Slowly the red-tiled roofs vanished into darkness, and electric lights came to life like a string of gems scattered over a dark velvet carpet.

I had only one evening to spend in Graz and most probably will never again get a chance to visit Graz or to gaze at its twilight beauty from the top of its beloved Schlossberg, but that one evening in Graz will stay embedded in my memory forever.

Spain: Barcelona and Catalonia

It was a beautiful copper sunset over the low hills surrounding Barcelona as the aircraft, having cruised over the Mediterranean Sea, touched down at El Prat Airport. It had been a delayed flight, and, despite my natural curiosity to experience and explore a new city and a new country, physical exhaustion had me looking forward to a warm bath, a clean bed and a silent room.

The first thing that strikes one about the Mediterranean coast is the warmth not only of the environment but also of the people and the ease with which life is lived. Here, there was no frantic rush of a London or even a New Delhi. People seemed to be simply living their lives from day to day. But then such initial impressions, especially made through the barrier of language, can often be misleading. As I strolled through the streets the next morning, I recalled that the same surrounding area had been the scene of a violent civil war in the previous century and had then endured several decades of dictatorship. Those days seemed far away from the peaceful environs of Ciutadella Park.

From the same harbour, bathed in a peaceful and even languid sunlight, in front of me Spanish 'conquistadores' had sailed to a distant America, bringing disease, death and destruction to a whole continent. The gilded ornamentation and riches that lay behind the cascading façades of the palaces owed their origin to the treasures and gold that had been brought back on those ships from the New World. Even today, as a reminder of those violent, greedy and unfortunate times, a huge pillar topped with a statue of Christopher Columbus, pointing beyond the sea, dominates the marina. Somewhere nearby, this gentleman, a native of Genoa, must have been received by the king and queen of Spain on his return from his historic journey. The reason he had first sailed was to find a different sea route to India, my homeland. He had accidentally 'discovered' the Americas, and how that accidental discovery has changed the world since then!

As I walked past the crowded La Rambla, the major touristic thoroughfare in Barcelona, on that sunny afternoon, I found it to be full of touristy kitsch: pavement artists, souvenir shops, cafés and eateries and all the other usual sights that today fill up the 'tourist hotspots' all over the world. But as I entered the maze of the old city nearby and came face-to-face with the pale yellow façades of the government buildings and cathedrals, I was suddenly reminded of my visit to Bogotá years ago and how its Spanish conquerors had sought to recreate a similar architecture, religion and an entire civilization on a distant land, miles across the Atlantic Ocean. Perhaps the ancestors of the Spanish students, laughing and enjoying the sun that afternoon on the roundabout, in front of me had been responsible for it. The old parts of Bogotá, I realized, was virtually a miniature of any large medieval Spanish city. Only that it was situated on the 'wrong' side of the Atlantic.

Having lived in India and having grown up on a steady and staple diet of English books and Hollywood movies, one tends to develop a narrow, Anglocentric view of the world. But as one travels, if one gets the chance to, that is one realizes that there are swathes of the globe where English is not even understood, much less spoken, and that one may travel for weeks from South America to China before encountering a single word of English and that there were long centuries when these parts had dominated the world. Today, except maybe in football Spain no longer dominates the world in any other field, but I was curious to know how the sediments of history affected the topography of a modern Spanish mind.

I asked Gabriel. Gabriel had studied in the local university and since then, plagued by the high unemployment that had become endemic to Spain following the 2008 Crisis, had been doing a series of temporary jobs, the most recent being that of an amateur tourist guide. He may not have been representative of a modern Spanish youth, as he was exceptionally well-informed and aware of most things—from the 'El Classico' match of the previous night, wherein his beloved Barcelona Football Club had lost to Real Madrid CF, to the voices of Catalonian separatism that showed itself in many a nook and corner of the city.

'We didn't learn anything from our history,' said Gabriel about the Spanish Civil War that dominated international politics and intellectual imagination in the thirties, of the last century. 'The wounds are still open, even if a bit below the visible surface,' he said, referring to the prevalent antagonism between the Spanish Left and Right that had once triggered those ghastly years of violence, when Hemingway, Orwell and a host of other liberal souls had come from all over the world to fight on the streets of Spain against what they thought were the forces of fascism, only to be disappointed and disillusioned later. 'The Spanish people have never come to terms with their past, unlike Germany, for example,' Gabriel added as we sat sipping sangria in a sun-drenched tapas bar on Piazza Catalonia, in the heart of the touristy city. Tulips and lavender bushes were gently swaying in a breeze that had brought a misty spray to our faces from the nearby fountain. Peoples from different cultures, races, languages and colours were milling around: Arabs with their ladies covered from head to toe, American college students basking in the sun and African vendors selling watches and trinkets on the pavement. I seemed to be the only Indian around.

As I sat talking to Gabriel about everything from Gabriel Garcia Marquez, who had died the previous day, to Pablo Picasso's paintings, I suddenly heard the faint tune of 'Auld Lang Syne' wafting through the air. A Chinese, as I found out later, was playing his violin, in the centre of Piazza Catalonia, to the tune of a song that was written hundreds of years ago in the misty, green Scottish Highlands by Robert Burns and had touched me, an Indian, with its universal appeal, defying the distance of space and time. Sometimes, during one's travels, one comes across such a sudden revelation that connects us all, across barriers of languages, distances, races and immigration desks, and that to me is the very essence and joy of travelling.

Barcelona owes much to Antoni Gaud and his architectural masterpieces, as my guidebook would like me to believe, and his shockingly bizarre and sensational façades are a source of curiosity for hordes of tourists all year round. But to me Barcelona is far more historical, far richer culturally, and is a far more complex mosaic of different influences, from Roman to Moorish to American.

Later I took a funicular up to the hills of Montjuïc, to look at the sunset over the sprawling city spread below, surrounded by low hills on three sides and the wide blue sea on one. The 1992 Olympic Stadium stood behind me and young men wearing Barcelona football jerseys were pranking around. As the sun went down and the sky darkened, the lights of the city slowly revealed themselves, one by one, and I was reminded of how I had looked down at Dehradun from the mall at Mussoorie, years ago, thousands of miles away. Columbus could never reach India, but the globe had indeed turned full circle.

From Thames to Seine

Charles Dickens begins his immortal *A Tale of Two Cities* with a vivid description of a journey from London to Paris, as it was during the last few years of the eighteenth century: horse-drawn carriages moving through rough, mud-splattered paths with ever-present dangers of robbery; crossing the Channel at Dover on a ferry and then onwards from Calais, through the French countryside, to Paris. Today the journey from London to Paris takes less than two-and-half hours on the high-speed Eurostar trains that swish past the warehouses, cars, rolling fields and farms and cross the sea through the 'chunnel' that goes underneath the sea; and before one can properly start to appreciate the journey the train eases into the Gare du Nord Station in Paris. The station, and especially its richly carved stone façade, is a throwback to a different era, an era when the railways have barely started its operation between the two cities. Although today the journey is fast and convenient, one does miss the white cliffs of Dover and crossing the Channel on an old P&O boat, as it was in olden times, but then one can't have both the worlds. In some ways, the journey in a Eurostar is like moving in an airtight, sanitized plane that moves on the ground and occasionally below the ground level.

Nicolas, my co-passenger, was studying English literature in Sheffield University and was going back to his home in Le Mans for the Easter vacation. He was visibly eager to get back home—his family of mother, brothers and niece, his friends, to a familiar environment where he would once again hear his beloved mother tongue. The carriage was symptomatic of how cosmopolitan the international tourist class had become—an old Chinese tourist, a modern Bangladeshi family, a retired American couple, a single English mother and her three daughters, an Arab family. But it was too short a journey for the strangers to overcome their inhibitions and to get to know their fellow travellers. So the 'other' remains the 'other', and an opportunity is lost—the journey becomes a mere physical displacement from one city to another.

If London is cool, convenient and comfortable to live in, Paris is exciting, energetic and a bit chaotic. In London every driver stops at a red light. In Paris many nonchalantly cross if they think there is no danger. And that difference in attitude is evident in many other ways.

My hotel, near the Place de la Règublique, was named without much imagination as Règublique Hôtel, and its claim to fame were the posters of Hollywood actors of a bygone era and it being the proud owner of the smallest elevator ever manufactured anywhere in the world. But then Parisian hotels have always taken advantage of its location in Paris.

The evening was cool, and there was a lovely breeze as I reached the lively Place de la Règublique, a square adorned with a stone-and-bronze monument commemorating the famous values of the French Revolution—equality, liberty and fraternity, something akin to the Statue of Liberty in New York, if not in size then in spirit. It was a weekend evening, and all the café pavement chairs were full. People of all ages and persuasions were out to enjoy conversations with friends, watch people walk by, enjoy the breeze and the moment in time; the art of doing nothing and enjoying the present.

Soon I was on the banks of the Seine River. By any measure, the Seine is an unremarkable river, but Paris has made it world-famous and immortal. The beauty for which Paris is justly famous is most visible from the banks of the Seine, and most of Paris's most impressive monuments—the Cathedral of Notre-Dame de Paris, Eiffel Tower, the Louvre, Arc de Triomphe are visible from the banks and bridges of the Seine. I had come to Paris six years ago, but Paris did not seem to have changed at all, or at least that was my impression during that introductory stroll along the river on my first evening in Paris six years later.

I could not detect any signs of change in the city. Even the trees along the Champs-Elysees seemed to be of exactly the same proportions. The cars wheezing past the Place de la Concorde, the Eiffel Tower shimmering at sunset, the boats carrying tourists from Pont Neuf to Eiffel Tower—all seemed to be the same as they had been recorded in the memory reel of my mind on my last visit. But thank God Paris had not changed, because it was difficult to improve upon its sheer beauty. I realized that I had nearly forgotten how impossibly beautiful Paris was as a city. Standing on the banks of Seine, looking at the series of architectural marvels—the Louvre, the royal palaces, the Conciergerie (a former prison) and the rest, I suddenly realized that this beauty and opulence was the result of oppression and inequality, of imperialism and exploitation and that what is beauty and magnificence for one is a symbol of decadence and suppression for another. But that I believe is true for most man-made wonders of the world, of the ancient and medieval world, and perhaps it is too harsh to judge the people, actions and events of one era by the values of another.

In DDLJ Country

It is generally recommended that one travel on the so-called 'Panoramic Express', from Montreux, on the banks of Lake Geneva, to Bern and then to Interlaken, in order to the world experience famous mountain railway of Jungfrau and travel up to the 'top of Europe'. However the views from my Geneva–Lausane–Bern–Interlaken journey were equally panoramic, and at a lesser cost. The views of the steel grey–blue Lake Geneva, with the overhanging Alpine peaks against a clear azure sky, gave way after Lausane to vineyards, apple orchards and pristine, green meadows dotted with belled cows. It was as if the days of Heidi had come back to life.

But the Switzerland of the days of Heidi and Mark Twain had changed vastly and irreversibly; modern technology, travel, prosperity and tourism had changed the face of the country, where superfast trains zipped through the countryside that had stayed in it splendid isolation for hundreds of years.

The contrast was complete as I approached the sprawling industrial suburbs of Bern, which must be one of the least-known and least pretentious capitals of the world. I could see the inevitable warehouses of famous multinational companies, modern cars and signs of the Big Mac. The only pointer that I was indeed in Switzerland, and not in any other international city in the First World was the advertisement billboards with the smiling face of Roger Federer on them.

If Bern is a little mundanely efficient and, therefore, a little characterless, Interlaken, despite being common in the tinerary of budget travellers, backpackers and adventure sports enthusiasts, manages to retain its charm. As the name suggests, Interlaken is the land between two large Alpine lakes Thun and Brienze, which may have been one in some remote geological age. A small channel of river called Aar connects the two lakes, and the town of Interlaken is spread around this river, with a railway line and a road running parallel to it. As my train eased into the Interlaken Ost Railway Station, its terminal point, I was instantaneously reminded of the railway station scene in the ironic Hindi movie of my youth, *Dilwale Dulhania Le Jayenge* (DDLJ), wherein Kajol, the heroine, misses her train and so begins her journey with Shahrukh Khan, the hero, through the picture-postcard countryside of Switzerland. I don't know whether Ost was indeed the same railway station, but it could very well be.

Interlaken, on a clear sunny day, is a beautiful and peaceful town to explore (especially if you are not committed to boarding the pre-booked Jungfrau mountain railway or to do one of the myriad adventure sports). A slight breeze was blowing over the surface of the river and was rustling through the leaves of a solitary Himalayan Pine which revived a distant memory of some other day, back in India. There were Indian restaurants with tricolour flags trying to attract Indian tourists, but their menus were written in Persian-Urdu script, a sure giveaway of their Pakistani owners. Outside India the artificially created boundaries between India, Pakistan and Bangladesh tend to lose their meanings, and all South Asians come to be categorized as one—belonging to a larger Indian subcontinent. However, I, despite my innate sense of loyalty to anything remotely Indian, had no desire an Indian meal that day.

We sat down in a terrace café, directly opposite the lovely green patch that lay at the centre of Interlaken, with the three snow-covered peaks of Eiger, Mönch and Jungfrau shining under the bright sun like the trident of Lord Shiva. Such ethereal beauty makes a man look towards the heavens and beyond; and just as Hindu places of pilgrimage are situated on the Himalayas—Kailash, Amarnath, Badri, Kedar—so also, for hundreds of years, Interlaken and its surroundings were owned and ruled by the monastery that stood before me. It was from here that the monks, the ultimate repository of all earthly and heavenly authority, dispensed wisdom and justice. Today the church building remains as a mute reminder of those long-forgotten days of watermills and sheep flocks sometime in the Victorian era, before the tourists arrived.

As is so often the case, the power of the written word made Interlaken famous, as Lord Byron and Goethe 'discovered' Interlaken and, impressed by the then virgin beauty of the place, told the world about it. Soon hordes of tourists came trooping into Interlaken, creating a boom of hotels. Some of those hotels still stand flanking the main street of the town, row renovated, but carrying silent stories in their hearts of an age long gone. And then came the railways, first from Bern to Interlaken and then, in a moment of spectacular engineering ambition and achievement, to Jungfrau; and as had happened in many a place on earth, everything changed.

But nostalgia for those nineteenth-century days is not for me, as in those days of colonialism and class inequality, a person like me, a middle-class Indian, would scarcely have got the opportunity to enjoy that sun-drenched terrace or a delicious potato rosti and cheese fondue served by an eager Swiss steward. Much of the nostalgia for the Victorian and Georgian days, in the collective minds of certain people in Britain, arises perhaps from a subconscious sense of loss of their empire or their pre-eminence on the world stage. Many a symbol of that age, such as the kitsch horse-drawn carriage, are sought to be preserved as a certain 'European way of life'. But then no age in history is completely dark or bright: the good and bad, the cruel and kind, the racist and enlightened, the regressive and progressive—they have co-existed as they do even now.

Lyon: The Gastronomical Capital of France

The dominance of Paris in French life has been and continues to be an issue in France's politics, history and culture. But the country is much more than its capital, as beautiful as the latter is.

My TGV journey from Paris-Gare de Lyon railway station to Lyon was fast, convenient and as impersonal as all modern train journeys were. The passengers, engrossed in their own narrow lives, were busy with their laptops and mobiles and had no time to stare out of the windows, at the beautiful misty morning coming to life over the green and yellow fields, or to converse with their fellow passengers, and before one realized it, the train had entered Lyon Railway Station, covering more than 400 miles in mere two hours!

But the pace of the city of Lyon was in sharp contrast with that of the TGV with there was no hustle and bustle that makes up the lives of the great cities of the world. A walk along the narrow, cobblestone-paved, medieval streets of Old Lyon was charming and beautiful, without the hordes of tourists that throng the other more famous cities of Europe.

The restaurants and cafés were opening for the day, and tables and chairs were being laid out on the pavements to serve food and wine, for which Lyon is justifiably famous. Some of the old houses, in their colour and structure of their façades, gave a distinctly Italian impression, and Joan, my French companion, confirmed that, indeed, in medieval times a lot of wealthy merchants and bankers from northern Italy had settled down in Lyon.

Soon we were on the banks of River Saône, one of the two rivers that flow through and merge at Lyon, the other being the bigger and more famous, Rhône. There were permanently marooned boats on the River Saône, now acting as restaurants, that reminded me of a time when the Rhône had been the highway of international trade. Silks of Lyon had made by local weavers used to travel up and down the river to distant ports.

The city square of Lyon is dominated by a huge bronze statue of the horse-mounted sun-king, Emperor Louis XIV. It is believed that the sculptor committed suicide after making it, as he realized that he had made a mistake in his creation. From the city square, Bellecour, I could get beautiful views of the hill that dominated the city, topped by the imposing nineteenth-century church of Fourvière that appeared to bless Lyon. Joan informed me that, although the city already had had the St Jean Cathedral on the banks of the river, the people then were so scared of the cholera epidemic that was sweeping through France that they promised they would build a new church to Virgin Mary if they were spared. And so today the Basilica of Notre-Dame de Fourvière stands as proof of both Lyon escaping the epidemic and its citizens fulfilling their promise. Later, when I took the century-old funicular train to the top of the hill and visited the basilica, its interiors appeared as remarkable as its story of origin. Light filtering in through the tall stained-glass windows showed Roman–Byzantine- style mosaics of coloured and golden tiles, which depicted scenes from Christian mythology on the high-vaulted Gothic ceiling. I had never before seen such an ornamental Gothic cathedral.

By this time, I was feeling famished, having left Paris early in the morning without having breakfast. We chose a typical local eatery that overlooked the city below, with the twin rivers meandering through to their confluence and the distant Alps on the horizon. The menu was all written in French, and I was more than content to let Joan make sense of it. She ordered a local dish called raclette—hot, molten, rich cheese poured over boiled potatoes. I liked it, if not for anything else, but for its exotic nature and the setting of the meal. The sun, the food, the view, the sound of the church bells, the fragrance of flowers wafting in from the road-side flower beds—all combined to make it a lovely afternoon, and I could understand why Joan, a loyal Lyon resident all her life, complained about the fast pace of Paris.

Joan was justly proud of her city and was happy about my curiosity about it. Although I had travelled by train to Lyon, I had learnt that the airport of Lyon had been named after Antoine de Saint-Exupéry.[5] In my youth, I had read the famous book *The Little Prince* by this pilot, writer and philosopher, and I was naturally curious to know more about him. Joan knew that de Saint-Exupéry belonged to Lyon but

---

5 Antoine Marie Jean-Baptiste Roger, Comte de Saint-Exupéry was a French writer, poet, aristocrat, journalist, and pioneering aviator.

was not aware of any museum or any such thing dedicated to him or his writings. But she told me that Lyon did have a museum on the Lumière brothers, as it was here in Lyon, in 1895, that the Lumière brothers made the first-ever film, *The Crowd Coming out of Factories*—an event to which all of Hollywood and Bollywood, from the Oscars to *Filmfare*, owe their origin. Joan had travelled to India more than a dozen times and, through her visits and extensive reading on India, mostly in French translations, knew more about India than many Indians. She was not an uncritical fan of India, and she did not feel any need to prove her loyalty and love for India. We finished off with Riz au lait, a rice-based dessert that appeared to be quite close to *our* own kheer.

Later, while taking a leisurely walk round the lake, in the sprawling gardens, as the shadows lengthened and the birds came chirping back to their nests, she shared some of her experiences from and impressions of India over the years— Pushkar, Agra, Almora, Darjeeling, Mandu, Kashmir—and her most recent visit to Maheshwar, the holy city on the banks of River Narmada, famous for its saris, among other things. I was somehow reminded of another person from Lyon, Claude Martin, soldier of fortune, who had been born in Lyon sometime in the eighteenth century, but who had worked in India, in then Calcutta and Lucknow. Today the La Martinère schools stand in his memory in Lyon, Kolkata and Lucknow. In a curious way Claude Martin had connected in his life to three cities that were also connected, somehow, to me.

The Decline, Fall and Rise of Pisa

Often, in today's age of pre-bookings over the internet and discounts for early bookings, our travel plans are made up weeks, and sometimes months, in advance. Gone are the days when one travelled with no advance reservations, only on the hope that one would get a hotel room or a train berth over the counter. But what one has gained in terms of convenience, security and economy, one somehow has lost in spontaneity, adventure and excitement—three hallmarks of travel.

And so my on, the, spur decision to take a detour to Pisa from Florence was something extraordinary. Apart from the Leaning Tower of Pisa, about which *we* all had read in our childhood as one of the Seven Wonders of the World, I was attracted by the prospect of travelling through the sun-drenched Tuscan countryside. Months ago, in my Lucknow apartment, on a lazy Sunday afternoon, I had watched the Hollywood movie *Under the Tuscan Sun*, and somehow the gold, green, blue and sunny memories of the movie had got embedded in the eyes of my mind. It was nice to find that, apart from the American, European and Australian tourists that usually made up the bulk of English-speaking tourists, we had two Indian couples travelling in the group. Meeting Indian tourists in the major tourist cities of the world was becoming increasingly common, and I had found them in London, Paris, Rome, Istanbul and almost everywhere else. Many of them form part of the huge dollar-earning diaspora that now inhabits every corner of the earth. Many belong to my generation, who had decided, due to whatever reasons, to make their homes away from home.

The coach snaked through the Tuscan countryside, past centuries-old small towns, with their church bell towers jutting out above, and an occasional ruined castle, still guarding the gateways to the fertile valleys. The trees were different—olive and maple; the flowers, lavender and tulips; and the people were speaking in a different language; but the sun, the light, and the sky appeared to be just like in my country.

Soon we were meandering along the banks of River Arno, the same river that we had seen in Florence, to enter Pisa. The river not only connects Florence and Pisa but also has changed the history and fortunes of these cities over the centuries. Hundreds of years ago, when Arno used to flow into the sea nearby, its riverine harbour was the source of the maritime prosperity of Pisa and its surrounding areas. Over the years, the harbour and the river silted up, and the sea moved miles away and took with it the fortunes of the city. There were similar instances throughout the course of history, from the Indus Valley Civilization to Ephesus to Alexandria. Who knows what will happen to the fortunes of the mighty cities of today—London, New York, etc.—a thousand years from now.

Today, after centuries of decline, Pisa has once again become prosperous, mainly due to tourism. As I entered the so-called Square of Miracles, actually the square of the cathedral or duomo, I saw scores of tourists in caps, holding their umbrellas, clicking photos of the famous Leaning Tower of Pisa that stood in front of me, leaning at a precarious and an almost miraculous angle. But apart from the gravity-defying and jaw-dropping angle, the Tower, actually the bell tower or campanile of the cathedral was in itself a uniquely beautiful architectural structure. I had never before seen such a multi-tiered bell tower, with arcaded columns of marble spiralling all the way up to the top. I could see tourists waving from the top to their partners below. Although the world-famous Tower is the centre of attraction, it is merely a bell tower of the centuries-old cathedral that stood nearby, which along with the baptistery makes up the third monument of the square.

The Cathedral of Pisa, naturally, has the same architectural features as its more famous bell tower, and its marble-clad, more-than-eight-centuries-old façade rose above me in stepped tiers with arcaded marble pillars adorning each tier, in a fashion that I couldn't remember having seen anywhere else in Europe. Although it does not look that old, the fact is that it predates the Duomo of Florence, the St Peter's Basilica of Vatican and, of course, the Gothic Duomo of Milan. The whole Square of Miracles looks preserved by the invisible hand of history and reminds *us* of a Pisa that was once very different. Curiously, half of the dome of the cathedral is clad in lead and the other half with tiles. The interiors are as richly carved, painted, ornamented and gilded as any of the most famous baroque churches of Italy.

Sometimes I wonder what prompted the popes and bishops to spend enormous amount of riches, time and effort on embellishing the houses of God, while the teachings of His Son were, who had decided to be born as a poor shepherd, had been to be frugal and simple. Was this a way to convince God of their devotion, a way to impress and even to awe the populace into mental subjugation, a way to patronize men of art—all of these, none of the above? Here in Pisa, the magnificent cathedral was made possible by the enormous loot that Pisa gained after ransacking a southern city-state of Italy, and the Byzantine golden mosaics and altarpieces were made up of the blood and hunger of a people now lost in memory. Somehow, the façade of the cathedral as well as the multi-tiered interiors of the baptistery, with its enormous water tub and intricately carved pulpit, reminded me of what little I had seen of Constantinople, now Istanbul, that was the capital of the eastern Roman Empire and of the whole Christian world for over a millennium. Today, of course, Istanbul is an almost wholly Islamic city of Turkey, but for almost a millennium, after the fall of Rome, it had been both at the centre of and at the vanguard of the Christian world, a millennium during when Hagia Sophia had been the largest church in the world, much before the present St Peter's Basilica had been constructed.

Maybe one day centuries ago, a baby named Galileo Galilei had been baptized in that very baptistery, in that very marble water tub, and then been led through the 'gates of paradise', to that very cathedral that stood in front of me. Galileo taught in the University of Pisa, one of the oldest in the world that stands even today. Later, his relations with the church became strained due to his iconoclastic and revolutionary theories in an age when the authority of the clergy had been much more than it is possible to imagine today.

Later, as Pisa's harbours silted up and its fortunes declined, it was conquered by Florence, by then the epicentre of Renaissance, and was reduced to a dependency and a mere suburb of the latter. The main gate to the cathedral square was permanently blocked; the white lion that had stood on top of the gate was made to face towards the city, and the pride of the city, Square of Knights, was completely redesigned to suit the fancy of the victors. And so, Pisa, with its magnificent cathedral and tower, languished for centuries under innumerable full moon nights, until one day, thanks to its greatest architectural folly, tourists of the modern world turned in its direction and stood once again at its portal; the skies opened up and the Tuscan sun once again cast its benign rays on the city.

The Most Beautiful City in the World

All great cities of the world have many facets to their personalities and choose to reveal only that facet that an onlooker or traveller wants to see. But probably the real essence and nature of a city is revealed only to those who are not seeking to see anything probably and that is, why it takes ages to really understand a place and its people. But even then one makes the mistake of making generalizations and simplifications. That is a danger or handicap that every traveller has to, be conscious of.

I had visited Paris, too before and on each such occasion it had appeared to me more beautiful than before. I had not been able to venture to Montmartre on any of those occasions. So that Sunday, while Paris was still waking up sleepy eyed, after overnight weekend parties, I trudged up from Place de la République to Montmartre. At the heart of the area stood, dominating entire Paris and affording the most panoramic view of the city, the Basilica of the Sacred Heart of Paris, more commonly known as Sacré-Cœur, with its unique elongated round dome of whitewash limestone and slender pillars.

In many ways, this church was very different from the grand dame of all churches in Paris, the Cathedral of Notre-Dame, from which most churches in not only Paris but also all of France got their inspiration. The basilica of Sacré-Cœur appeared to be as different from Notre-Dame as its Bohemian surroundings of artists and freethinkers were different from the aristocratic surroundings of Notre-Dame. While the interiors of the basilica, with its vaulted roof and stained-glass windows were beautifully Gothic in an unspectacular sort of way, its location on a raised hill and its beautiful white dome flanked by minaret-like towers made Sacré-Cœur remarkable.

As I walked on the narrow cobblestone pathways surrounding the church, which were slowly filling up with Chinese tourists led by a Chinese-speaking, umbrella-wielding European guide, I realized that Paul Cézanne or Van Gogh, or maybe Sartre or Proust might once have walked in on these pavements, and had coffee at the same La Bohème café that faced me. Today, on these same lanes, scores of old artists dot the pavements, peddling their art to tourists at ridiculously low prices, bowing their heads in front of the goddess of necessity and commerce and yet continuing to serve the goddess of art.

But, despite the Bohemian eccentricities of Montmartre and the out-of-way beauty of Sacré-Cœur, the pride of place as the prima donna of all churches in France must surely belong to the Cathedral of Notre-Dame, which stands in the middle of an island that divides the Seine into two. This huge and exquisite medieval, Gothic church, with its signature double rectangular towers and large glass windows dominating its façade, has been the lifeline of the religious and cultural Paris from the medieval ages to this day. I was fortunate that, on that Lent Sunday, the choir was singing, and despite the fact that I couldn't understand a single word of what was being sung, I felt I understood the essence and feeling behind the soulful rendering that boomed in the vaulted enclosed space of the church. Stylish, well-dressed, modern Parisians were listening to the sermon being given by a dark-skinned priest who stood at the pulpit. Tourists like me from all over the world milled around silently, observing the paintings, stone carvings of long-dead priests and saints, beautiful chapels made in recesses and sarcophagi of holy men who were eminent in their time. As I wandered through, I was reminded of how the same Cathedral of Notre-Dame, tall, noble and proud against the blue sky of Paris, had been a silent witness, over the centuries, to aristocratic oppression and violent revolutions, periods of alternating order and chaos, progress and decline and hope and despair.

Probably the best way to take in the essential sights of Paris in a short time is to take a boat cruise on the River Seine, from the Eiffel Tower to the Cathedral of Notre-Dame and beyond, as most of the beautiful monuments of the city are located on either banks of the river. The impressive façade of the Louvre, once a royal palace, but today a world-famous museum, with the modernistic glass pyramid at its entrance contrasting sharply with its medieval stone façade, with innumerable statues of men once famous, dominates the left bank. On the opposite bank stands the Musée d'Orsay, once a railway station, with the names of various destinations still carved on its stone façade, but today, again, a world-famous museum, as does the palace where, during the peak of French

Revolution, Queen Marie Antoinette was kept in captivity.

As one's boat glides, almost noiselessly, underneath the beautiful bridges, from Pont Neuf to Pont Alexandre III, one can see Parisians waving, or sitting and idling, on the banks of the river, enjoying a leisurely and sunny late summer. By the time my boat deposited me back in front of the Eiffel Tower, after an hour-long trip, I felt my senses had been saturated with beauty, if that was possible.

There is something about the Eiffel Tower and its inexplicable attraction. In a city with such exquisite marvels as the Notre-Dame, Louvre, Napoleon's Tomb, Arc de Triomphe and others, this gigantic structure of riveted wrought-iron and steel, erected, not so long ago as the city goes, mainly as a gate to an exhibition, has become such a universal symbol of the city that more than anywhere else in Paris international tourists congregate in front of the Eiffel Tower, to get themselves photographed and to promptly upload to on it their Facebook pages. Nowhere else in Paris did I see so many Indian honeymoon couples as here, a sign of Indian middle classes' recently acquired affluence and mobility. There were also numerous African and Bangladeshi vendors, as in other tourist sports Europe, selling cheap souvenirs to foreign tourists. It appeared to me that the Parisians themselves had turned their backs on a monument that, to their great surprise, became a symbol of their city.

It was a beautiful sunny day and the 'real' Parisians were out in number, away from the tourist spots, in the gardens and parks, enjoying the sun and peace. They didn't feel the need to cover the entire tourist trail in a couple of days, to get themselves photographed, to shop for souvenirs or see the 'sights'. They were simply living their lives, one day at a time, in the most beautiful city in the world. I wondered whether they thought themselves to be as lucky as I had imagined them to be. Maybe some did, maybe others didn't. A vagabond traveller can only wonder and move on.

Under the Real Tuscan Sun

As my train first climbed up the Alps and then jutted through the long, dark tunnels drilled through its bellows, I emerged from Switzerland into Italy, into the bright luminosity of a completely different landscape. Here, although the countryside looked a little ramshackle and run-down compared to Switzerland, it looked more natural and wild.

Six years ago, I had travelled in the opposite direction, by road, across the Italy–Swiss border, where Swiss policemen had gone through our passports and visas. In those days Switzerland had not yet agreed to be a member of the Schengen one visa regime. I remembered that the road through the Alps had passed through much more picturesque and more spectacular vistas—through snow-covered peaks and mountainsides. Or maybe, the passage of time had made the memories grow fonder.

After briefly passing through some picture-postcard Alpine villages along the coast of a placid but beautiful lake, the train took us hurtling down south into the heartland of a sunnier Latin land. It was impossible to imagine that the peaceful and lazy landscape that was flying past the windows of the train had indeed been the land of brutal battles and atrocities in the days of *A Farewell to Arms*. It must have been in these villages that a young and romantic Hemingway would have come across the stark realities of World War I, as well as the sweet illusions of his first love.

The atmosphere within the carriage had changed too since we had crossed the international border, and lively, noisy Italian passengers were laughing and talking in Italian, with the unmistakable *o* added to every second word. Large families and friends, decidedly from their northern European neighbours, were travelling together. After a change of train in Milan—no time for the duomo or La Scala this time—I found myself travelling under the setting Tuscan sun, on my onward journey to Florence. The flat countryside outside the Trenitalia window resembled, at least from a distance, the rural landscape of Punjab in India. Isolated clumps of village houses, a tractor belching dust, sparkling canal waters, electricity towers and poles flew past me. Only the occasional bell tower of a church broke my trance as the train sped past Bologna towards Florence. One of my fellow passengers was from Napoli, and what he lacked in his command over English he more than made up for with his sincere and apparent warmth. He had never travelled to India but had managed to go to Mauritius, where he had witnessed what he thought was an extended Indian culture. He bid me a warm farewell as our train eased into Florence, or Firenze, as it is universally called in Italy, into the Santa Maria Novella Station.

A traveller merely passing through a place invariably will miss out on many of the place nuances and can never claim to know all and should therefore be wary of making strong opinions and generalizations based on that fleeting visit. That said, the three most notable impressions that Florence made on me were the Renaissance, Christianity and the tourists. It was the city where the Renaissance—in literature, in art, in architecture and, most importantly in thought—not only had been born but also had flourished as in no other city. But what had supported the works of a Dante, or that of a young Michelangelo or a Leonardo da Vinci had been the tremendous wealth of its rich merchant families. The most important of these families had been the House of Medici, whose presence could still be felt in Florence, even after so many centuries. Here, in these very narrow, stone-paved lanes and by-lanes had lived and walked Dante Alighieri; Here, he had written his immortal *Divine Comedy* and had met, loved and longed for his Beatrice, before being permanently exiled from his beloved city.

Today, tourism has embraced Dante; and hordes of American and Chinese tourists, many of them holding a Dan Brown novel, paid their obligatory respects to the house where the famous poet supposedly had been born many centuries ago. Cafés and bars, all using the famous poet's name, crowded the tiny house and church from all sides, and suddenly I felt curious about the lives and feelings of these ordinary Florentine people, who live today behind the façades of these historic buildings. Were they grateful for living in such historic quarters, were they irritated by the crowd and noise of the tourists, or were they just indifferent, having got used to all these scenes since birth?

Long queues of tourists stood every morning in front of the Uffizi Gallery that houses supposedly the finest collection of Renaissance paintings anywhere in the world and also in front of the Academic Gallery that houses the famous marble statue of David by Michelangelo, probably the finest and most famous piece of Western sculpture anywhere in the world. But Florence itself is a huge virtual open-air museum, with history, heritage and art plastered over every nook and corner.

But despite all the artistic and architectural gems of Florence, no building can probably hold a candle to the duomo, the massive central church with its signature russet-coloured dome that dominates the skyline of the city. But Florence is not merely a city of history but also very much a living city, and Catholicism is alive and kicking here even in the twenty-first century—something that cannot be said about many other cities of northern Europe. Deep in the moonlit night, as I stood sipping a glass of local Chianti at Piazza della Signoria, in front of the palace of the Medici family, I suddenly found a crowd of devotees, holding olive branches, candles and crosses, silently moving in a procession towards the church, in some unfathomable ancient ritual, about which even my local Italian waiter could not elaborate. But from the look on their faces, lit by candlelight, their faith and devotion were apparent, even without a single word being spoken.

The next morning, I was lucky again. I witnessed a more formal procession that started from the Baptistery (perhaps the oldest building in Florence today where Dante himself was supposedly baptized), and moved through the enormous ornamental brass gates (the gates of paradise), to the Duomo. There were priests of different countries and ages wearing white and purple robes and caps, holding olive branches and other ceremonial objects. I could see the unmistakable features of a priest from south India and that of a lady Chinese priest.

Today it is difficult to imagine the Duomo, literally meaning 'god's house', without its mind-boggling marble and stone façades, but my guidebook told me that the façade is of a comparatively recent, nineteenth-century antiquity. But undoubtedly the most impressive feature of the Duomo of Florence is the dome, with its massive size and proportions towering over everything in the city. Compared to its façade, the interior of the cathedral is somewhat less spectacular, except for the rich paintings on the roof depicting various scenes from Christian mythology.

Scores of tourists were milling around the dome and bell tower clicking away to glory, eager to update their Facebook statuses. But if the old American tourist couples and groups of Chinese tourists, swarming through the Duomo and the Uffizi Gallery, and the bands of young students offering free 'hugs' were one facet of Florence of today, the Bangladeshi hawkers, selling knick-knacks in front of the Duomo trying to make a living, separated from their families and homelands by thousands of miles and innumerable immigration barriers, told another story, if only one cared to stop and listen. I couldn't be indifferent to them, and even if I knew that I couldn't do anything to change the situation, my helplessness at the inequity and injustice, invisible to all, gnawed at me. Maybe I felt closer to them linguistically, racially and culturally.

Later I walked over the Ponte Vecchio, the only medieval bridge over River Arno that survived; the rest were bombarded away during the violent days of World War II. Today, the bridge is lined on both sides by world-famous watch and jewellery stores, as it has been for centuries. I was more curious about the famous concealed corridor created by Vasari, the favourite architect of the Medici family. This corridor runs all along the bridge, connecting the two palaces that stand at its entire ends. I had of course read Dan Brown's *Inferno*, as had all the American tourists who were looking up to the corridor from the bridge below.

Florence is beautiful, in a way very few cities of the world can compare. But the most beautiful sight of Florence is the sunset over the city, as seen from Piazza Michelangelo, high up on the south bank of River Arno. As soon as I climbed up to it, I could recognize the Florence of numerous picture postcards and documentaries, with the looming, orange–russet dome of the Duomo catching the last rays of the sun and the series of bridges, one after another, silhouetted against the silvery-golden surface of the placid river. The bells of the innumerable churches, of the medieval city of Boccaccio and Plutarch, of da Vinci and Dante, of Michelangelo and Medici, suddenly started ringing as they would have done in centuries past, calling the devout to the path of God. The electric lights slowly started coming to life; the sun began to sink; a breeze began to blow; and I somehow got a glimpse of the city that had inspired the Renaissance.

Up On the Swiss Alps

Though the favourite destination of many Indian tourists in Switzerland was undoubtedly the Jungfrau–Lucerne–Interlaken area, I decided to take a train journey to the small but popular mountain village of Zermatt in the south. Apart from the recommendations of my host, who had been living in Geneva for more than a decade, I tended to away from the common tourist trails and sights. So in Paris, I had never visited the Louvre and in Barcelona, I had avoided a visit to the large Roman Catholic church called the Basílica i Temple Expiatori de la Sagrada Familia. However, I had rarely regretted my chosen off-beat paths, and so was the case this time.

The highlight or at least one of the highlights, of any trip to Switzerland has to be the railway journeys. These are not the quaint little railway stations of eastern Europe, or the dusted neglect of an 'Old Patagonian Express' or the colourful chaos of the Indian railways. These are very Swiss—perfectly maintained, clean, fast, efficient and punctual, cutting across the magnificent Alpine scenery, promising and delivering world-class comfort. As my train skimmed through the coast of Lake Geneva and passed through picture-postcard towns of Nyon, Lausanne, Montreux, I could see the pinnacles of age-old castles and church spires, the houses of the rich and famous overlooking the lake and a Swiss cyclist going on a mountain hike. The snow-covered peaks of the Alps hangover the still and bluish-grey surface of the vast lake and provided a dramatic backdrop that was almost surreal in its beauty.

As the train moved away from the shores of the lake, the scene outside the wide windows changed, and I took a breather to look at my fellow travellers. Although Zermatt was a popular tourist destination, on that day, the carriage was mostly empty. Fred, my fellow passenger was Swiss-French and was on his way to Milan, where he lived and worked in a design studio and shared his flat with his British co-workers. I was surprised and pleased to know that he had already travelled to south India on a vacation a year ago, and was eager to visit India once again and see Agra and Varanasi. He appeared to be surprisingly well-informed about India and was a keen follower of the election scene that was unfolding at that time in the largest democracy in the world. Soon we found ourselves deep in conversation about topics like the then crisis of credibility of the Swiss banking system, the peculiarities of the Swiss political system and, of course, the greatest Swiss icon of my generation—Roger Federer. For a nation that did not promote any personality cult—and I could not remember any Swiss statesman or leader—Federer was clearly an exception as his face loomed from advertisement billboards and magazine covers all over Switzerland.

A change of train in Visp saw me on a mountain railway, with its peculiar rack and pinion system. I was now travelling through more rugged and more rustic mountain scenes with deep gorges and tiny hamlets that must have existed for hundreds of years with their rustic inhabitants grazing sheep on the mountainsides and a solitary church acting as a focal point of their lives. But then the railways and the tourists arrived. I was now travelling on the famous Glacier Express that runs through wild and white Siberia-like glaciers and tricks the traveller into imagining a polar scene but in the comfort and warmth of Swiss hospitality. As was expected, the first-class section had a special menu of choice food and drinks, but I had not expected to find a special Indian menu along with the standard international fare. It was a reflection of both the number of Indian tourists travelling to Switzerland every year and the care that the Swiss take to make them feel welcome.

The chief claim to fame of Zermatt lies in its being the starting point for mountaineering expeditions to the famous Matterhorn—a peak that has always cast a mysterious allure on mountaineers from all across the globe, much as a flame attracts moths. As the train panted up the steep incline through small, isolated stations—Stalden, St Niklaus, Täsch—I got glimpses of the famous peak at some odd bend and turn of the track. But Zermatt affords splendid and complete head-to-toe views of the Matterhorn from many vantage points, as I soon found out. The village appeared to be a typical starting point for mountaineering and skiing expeditions, with the inevitable skiers, equipment-renting shops, budget hotels, discotheques and kitsch.

I was reminded of the splendid views of Nanda Devi that I once had, from the tiny mountain resort of Auli, in the

Garhwal Himalayas. There are many mountain peaks, that are higher even in Switzerland, but somehow the Matterhorn, perhaps because of the combined effect of its shape, the legends associated with it, the mountaineering challenge that it poses and the marketing juggernaut that has adopted it to sell everything from vacations to chocolates, has become unique. As I walked up the crowded and pedestrianized central street of Zermatt, I could see the famous Monte Rosa Hotel, where the members of the legendary British expedition team had stayed before embarking on the first-ever successful summit attempt of the Matterhorn. It had turned out to be a tragic expedition when on the way down the rope had snapped and some of the more unfortunate ones had fallen to their certain deaths. To them the resplendent peak that stood before me and glittered in the sunlight must have looked sinister. A small museum in Zermatt displays the piece of rope that snapped on that fateful day in 1865, ending the lives of a few brave men.

For a timid, middle-aged traveller from India, skiing on the slopes of the Matterhorn or attempting to scale its dramatic heights was not an option, and so I took a journey on yet another funicular railway that started from Zermatt and wound its way up through unbelievably steep hikes and through wildly isolated railway stations and snow-covered scenes to its final destination, more than 3000 metres high. We were the only Indians, and the funicular railway that afternoon was full of European skiers of all ages, out to enjoy the Easter vacation with their families. The pinnacle of the journey was the dramatic 360 degree views from the viewpoint where the funicular railway finally ended its long haul. One could identify at least half a dozen more-than-4000 metre-high peaks including the Matterhorn, shining under the afternoon sun in its magnificent glory. As I stood at the viewpoint I saw a honeymooning Italian couple, an old Chinese man who was praying to each of the peaks, doing something like our own Suryanamaskar and a middle-aged British couple with their young family. The age-old beauty of divine nature seemed to awe everyone, even experienced travellers who had seen the world.

It is a sign of our commercial times that even at such heights a full-fledged hotel, restaurant or a shopping mall could be found. Hotel Klum's sun-drenched open, air restaurant was filled with sunglass-wearing, white faces of the rich of the world, who were soaking up the sun and nature and were perhaps revelling in their exclusivity and good fortune. Many of them had their expensive rooms booked in the hotel and would continue to watch the splendid sunset over the Alps, as the last rays of the sun would kiss the peaks of Matterhorn, long after the less fortunate travellers would have gone down on the last trip of the funicular railway. I could only imagine the ethereal beauty of the Matterhorn under a full moon as the funicular railway took me down to Zermatt. That magical image remained with me along with the *real* beauty of sunny afternoon. Sometimes the most beautiful memories in life are the ones in one's longings.

PART 3
Across the Straits

Memories of Morocco: The Atlantic's Roar at Casablanca

In the collective memory of the modern world Casablanca is more of a western European city, where Humphrey Bogart, with a cigar dangling from his lips, mumbled sweet nothings to Ingrid Bergman long back. And in many ways, Casablanca, although situated in Morocco and, therefore, in Africa, does retain a Southern European character, with its wide tree-lined boulevards, spacious city squares, shopping centres and good infrastructure. The highway that connects the airport, some thirty kilometres away, to the city centre was in excellent condition, and the transport, hotels and other facilities were far removed from the picture of Africa I had in my mind. There were cars and buses, excellent tramways, small 'petit' taxis—all uniformly coloured in red, cafés with French menus, wide roads with bright street lights, and the city and the country seemed to be thriving.

Situated near the Atlantic Ocean, at least as far as visual beauty goes. But before savouring the ocean, I decided to stroll through the heart of the city to get a feel of the place. I was curious and eager, as Casablanca was the first time I had encountered the tremendous continent of Africa. Although the city is not the capital of Morocco and is not considered an imperial city, it remains the country's largest city. At its heart, there is a large and impressive square, surrounded by imposing government buildings, built in an architectural fashion that show the influence of the French but are still not entirely French. Mohammed V Square, named after a former king of Morocco (the grandfather of the present king), is pleasant, leafy and wide, and I could make out the yellow-coloured façades of the law courts, the French Consulate and the Central Bank surrounding it from three sides. There were teenagers playing football in the square, over the pavements and, black-topped streets, and tall, old Moroccan men in brightly coloured full-length grabs were selling drinking water from goatskins, pouring the water into shining brass tumblers as their ancestors might have done in ages long gone by.

Although it was a Sunday, a weekly public holiday in a largely Muslim country, the old central market was open. Some Moroccan salesmen, always eager but not pestering, were selling fresh seafood—fish, crabs, oysters and prawns; others were selling olives and olive oil; some had huge tangerines and pomegranates; and the flower sellers had impressive stalls of irises, carnations and exotic flowers; but the most vocal were the tea shops serving a peculiar concoction of tea served with mint leaves and large lumps of sugar in tiny glass cups—a Moroccan speciality. I could see that the Moroccan people had retained, and were proud to retain, their distinctive cuisine, their signature products and avenues of enjoyment, and although there was a rare

McDonald's or Starbucks, it was their own local dishes and drinks that was served there.

Undoubtedly, the most impressive monument of Casablanca, and one of the most impressive I have seen anywhere, is the Hassan II Mosque, with its huge and intricately carved cuboidal stone minaret. The mosque, named after another former king, the father of the present one, is not old at all, and must rank as one of the largest and greatest mosques built anywhere in the world in the last century. Apart from its architectural symmetry, profusion of multicoloured mosaics and stone carvings, and the sheer size of the mosque and its courtyards, the setting of Hassan II Mosque was quite stunning—right on the edge the roaring Atlantic Ocean, with the waves lapping its edges during high tide. I don't know why such a fragile setting was chosen to build such a huge structure, that too in a land that has known seismic events in the past, but I am pretty sure that it must have some mysterious significance. From the single minaret of the mosque a laser light was visible in the night, pointed towards distant Mecca, probably as a reminder to the faithful about their religion and its source.

Walking along the ocean front of Casablanca, with the huge roaring waves of the Atlantic pounding on the embankment walls, through the maze of hawkers selling Moroccan breads, tea, savouries and cigarettes, with the massive Hassan II Mosque forming the backdrop, will be a memorable experience for anyone. Compared to this the site of the famous Casablanca Conference of 1942, held by the then superpowers at the height of World War II, to decide upon the future of the world, looked rather artificial and as ephemeral as the results of the Conference proved to be. Those men that day could not have imagined that the world around them was going to change so soon, and so irreversibly, and that 'Winston' would remain only as a name of a brand of cigarette being sold by Moroccan street vendors to tourists.

The site of the Conference was an otherwise unremarkable building, situated in the elitist and European part of the city, over a small hill called Anfa, and today nothing distinguishes it apart from its surrounding buildings.

As I stood atop the hill, looking at the hazy ocean in front of me, it struck me that nobody knew how the world of men would change in the coming years and centuries, and maybe one day the great men and cities of today would be merely a distant memory; but the Atlantic Ocean would keep roaring away under the same sky and the same sun.

I felt humbled and peaceful at the same time, and I bid adieu to Casablanca with this thought about man's impermanence in my mind and the sight of the soaring solitary minaret of the grand Hassan II Mosque in front of my eyes.

Memories of Morocco: The Imperial City of Fez

My guide was named Mohammad, as many men in Fez, or indeed in the whole Islamic world were. He was a tall, gaunt man, dressed in Jellabah (a common flowing head-to-foot dress of Arabs), and looked straight out of *Lawrence of Arabia*. Like him, the city of Fez seemed weathered yet timeless, dynamic and yet serene and layered yet harmonious.

Fez, the most ancient of the four imperial cities of Morocco, is also the city where the world-famous fez cap originated and spread, through the Ottomans, all across the globe. I had read somewhere that Kemal Atatürk had outlawed the wearing of fez, perhaps in his bid to radically westernize Turkey. But in fez I could see hawkers selling fez caps to tourists when we had driven up, early in the morning, to one of the castles that overlooks the city and affords excellent views of not only the city sprawled below but also the plains surrounding it that extends up to the distant hazy hills. The city of Fez, founded by the earliest sultans of Morocco, more than a millennium ago, has witnessed many upheavals in history and yet has managed to see them through and even today continues to live in an unbroken sequence of time in its ancient lanes and by-lanes, within the ramparts of its Medinas. As I could see from my vantage point, the city is divided into three neat parts; the older Medina—Fez el-Bali—and the newer but still some-seven-hundred-years-old Medina to the north; Fez el Jedid in the centre; and the modern Fez to the south that developed under the influence of the French and continues to, with its hotels and wide boulevards. All the three cities are situated close to each other, nestled between the low hills on all sides, which must have provided natural protection in the violent medieval era when the emperors of Morocco ruled from here. Even today, one can notice the medieval forts, all of the same beige-mud colour, situated on the hill tops guarding the passes below. Mohammad told me that the one in the south had been converted into a museum of arms and artillery but was visited more for the panoramic views of the city that it afforded.

One may do well to live in the new modern Fez, but the throbbing heart of the city can be seen and be felt only in its ancient Medina. It is believed to be the largest car-free urban zone in the whole world, and the only option to walking is to ride a mule through the narrow lanes. I, like most, decided on the former. The Medina of Fez must be very fascinating and exotic in the eyes of a European or an American traveller, but to me it felt like walking through a huge chowk and Aminabad of Lucknow combined into one. There were fruit sellers and butchers in their small hole-in-the-wall shops various noises and smells were all mixed up; and artisans worked on their clay pottery and stone mosaics as their ancestors did in centuries past. There were whole areas within the Medina where metal workers were hammering away to make pots, pans and artefacts, and I was reminded of similar sounds as artisans made silver foils in some other lane, in some other city; carpet weavers were weaving beautiful patterns and had combined modern business acumen and ancient artistic traditions. An entire area, a rather smelly one, was dedicated to the dangerous and hazardous-looking tannery pits of various chemicals and dyes, where workers were manually processing skins of camels and goats to produce modern leather apparels, to fill up the showrooms of New York, Paris, London and Milan. The prices, everywhere in Morocco, from a cheap taxi ride to an expensive carpet, were open to mind-boggling negotiations, and a standard marked price was an exception rather than a rule. It was a place for bargaining delight or sorrow, depending on which side you are on, but the bargaining was always done in good humour, with a smile and good cheer, as if it was all a game, not to be taken seriously. Each transaction was unique, a game of wit between two players, as if in a game of chess, and each time a new price was 'discovered'.

But if Fez el Bali is the heart of Fez, the ancient Koutoubia Mosque with its tall, cuboidal minaret and the adjacent madrassa, believed by many to be the most ancient university of the world, is the heart of Fez el Bali itself. Unfortunately, as in most of Morocco, the mosques and madrassas were not open to non-Muslims, and I had to content myself with the intricately carved wooden gate of the Mosque and the sound of the students repeating Arabic verses loudly. In places such as these one has to use the eyes of one's mind, one's imagination, to see a descendant of Ibn Batuta, studying perhaps in the same madrassa, studying the same scriptures as his medieval and globetrotting ancestors did once.

Both the Medinas, literally meaning ancient city, of Fez are ringed by thick walls, plastered with a beige-coloured mud-like substance and perforated with a series of pockmarked ventilation holes. Just as in *our* own walled city of Old Delhi, the walls of Fez too have a number of ornate gates, each with a name that has come down from the medieval ages, from centuries of mystical Arabian nights. Beyond the walls and the gates lie the remnants of a once thriving Jewish society, with its distinct religion, culture and architecture. The Jewish population of Fez has unfortunately dwindled to a very small number, mainly due to emigration, Mohammad told me, and today those quarters, tellingly situated outside the walls, with their first-floor wooden balconies overhanging the streets below, act as a mute testimony of a people, a culture and a society that has managed to survive like no other.

I don't know when and how Judaism arrived in Morocco, but before Islam arrived along with the Arabs from the east, Morocco was the natural habitat of a people, whom the world, taking after the ancient Romans, called 'Berbers'. The Romans came, conquered and vanished; the Arabs came, conquered and converted them to Islam; but the ancient Berber people, with their distinct culture, script and music survive to this day, living in apparent harmony, but distinct from the Arabs. Before coming to Morocco, I had not known about the Berber people, although unfortunately the word 'barbarian' that owe its origin here was known to all. My driver Mohammad was a Berber, and my guide, another Mohammad, was an Arab, but to my unaccustomed eyes it was difficult to tell the difference. But sometimes I wondered what the descendants of the ancient Berbers, self-aware of their culture and distinct history, thought and felt when they saw their world and land. Did they feel that they had been changed, had been conquered, had been converted or have been saved? None of the above? All of these?

Travelling is not only about monuments. It is not only about crafts; it is much more than beautiful landscapes. It is all of these and something more. Travelling is about the stories that make the land, the people and their creations, their lives, memories and dreams, and it is about what the traveller makes out of these—transforming them with his own perception and in turn transforming himself.

Memories of Morocco: Rabat, the Capital

I had always thought that Marrakesh was the capital of Morocco. But I was wrong. Morocco, for a country with a population of barely thirty-five million, has more than its fair share of famous cities. Apart from Marrakesh, it has Casablanca, its largest city, of Humphrey Bogart fame; it has the medieval city of Fez, from where, among other things, the world-famous fez caps originated; and on the Mediterranean coast, the ancient city of Tangiers. But none of them has the distinction and honour of being Morocco's political capital. That is reserved for the much lesser known city of Rabat.

To be honest, I had never even heard of Rabat before I had decided to make a trip to Morocco, but I am glad now that I included it in my journey. Apart from the city of Rabat, the smooth road journey from Casablanca, on a highway that could have been anywhere in Europe and that, for the most part, skirted the waves of the Atlantic Ocean on my left, against a backdrop of a reluctantly setting sun, provided for a very pleasant evening. Rabat is actually, as is so common in many a European city, one of a set of twin cities—Rabat and

Sale—divided and separated from each other by a river, Bou Regreg, which flows into the Atlantic Ocean here. I was lucky that my hotel was situated right on the banks of the river, with one of its many beautiful bridges, lit up at night, visible from my room. The city was is a pleasant blend of the medieval and modern, and one would come across medieval walls and ramparts right in the middle of modern, zipping traffic and gleaming tramways. There was a pleasant, cool breeze blowing from the ocean, and the city gave an impression of being modern, safe and cosmopolitan, and so despite the fact that it was late in the night by the time I had my dinner at the hotel restaurant, I decided to explore the city, or at least some parts of it, on foot.

Not only is Rabat one of the four medieval, imperial cities of Morocco, but it also remains, even today, the seat of power and home of the monarch, and in that sense it is the only Moroccan imperial city that continues to be so. The present king, Mohammed VI, a descendant of the Alaouite Dynasty that goes back to the 1600s, rules his kingdom from his royal palace in Rabat. There is precious little of the two-century- old royal palace that one can see, and I had to be content with looking at the impressive gate and façade of the palace and the royal guards dressed in a predominantly red uniform. The palace continues to be the seat of real power, unlike Buckingham Palace in London, despite some recent political reforms during the reign of the present king, who has chosen to live with his small family in his comparatively modest quarters outside the city. This may have been an attempt to separate the private from the public. I wondered how successful he was.

Medina literally means 'the old city' in Arabic and is usually surrounded by a wall. All imperial cities of Morocco have at least one such Medina, and although, compared to Fez and Marrakesh, the Medina of Rabat is not as big or as atmospheric, walking through the narrow lanes and by-lanes of the Medina of Rabat, along the mud-coloured massive medieval ramparts, is an experience that will affect the senses of any traveller. Next morning I walked through quaint-looking ancient wooden doors with the 'Hands of Fatima' knockers, which are considered auspicious, across tea shops serving super-saturated sweet tea with whole mint leaves in tiny glass tumblers and across small gardens where the youth of Rabat were playing music on common Middle-Eastern instruments. From a vantage point, I could see both the medinas—one on the Rabat side and the other one across the river on the Sale side with the Atlantic Ocean in front. Although today one may only encounter wide-eyed tourists and eager hawkers walking through these streets, there was a time when tall Berber and Arab soldiers had launched numerous military expeditions from behind these ramparts, on boats, across the ocean in front, to not-so distant Spain and Portugal.

A stark reminder of those lost medieval time is the Hassan Tower, which is the most dominant and most remarkable landmark of the present cosmopolitan city of Rabat. Although it was never actually completed, as its patron sultan expired before its completion, the rectangular minaret of the mosque still looms over the skyline of Rabat. Unlike the slender and cylindrical minarets of mosques in India or Turkey, here in Morocco, all the minarets were cuboidal and took after the earliest traditions of minarets in Islam from Palestine and

Syria, which themselves might have been derived from the towers of the churches they replaced. Even today the Hassan Tower continues to inspire the design and architecture of minarets of mosques and mausoleums all across Morocco.

Just across the street from the tower of Hassan lies the royal mausoleum of the modern twentieth-century kings of Morocco, the father and grandfather of the present king. The green-roofed building, although not very large, is a little gem of embellishment with intricate ornamentation from inside. It has beautiful marble flooring, intricate stone carvings and mosaics and carved cider wood of such great and harmonious beauty that it manages to amaze and awe even the most hardened and weary of world tourists. Despite its beauty and importance, I could not find many tourists that morning at the royal mausoleum, and apart from me there were only a few officials and royal guards, with their flowing uniforms and rifles that had beautiful stone inlay work on the wooden butt. I could spend as much time as I had wanted in the royal mausoleum and its peaceful courtyards and gardens with the Hassan Tower as the backdrop and the slowly flowing river down below, at a distance. Another frantic and busy working day of the modern capital city was coming to life, and the trams, buses and cars were crossing the bridge across the river, and yet the doves sitting on the ledges of the Hassan Tower continued to sit and coo, as the doves had perhaps been doing for the last eight centuries or so, watching the world change and yet remaining the same.

Turkish Delight: The One and Only Hagia Sophia

Istanbul is much more than the sum total of its monuments. Nevertheless, each of its many beautiful mosques and palaces can lay an undeniable claim to fame and has done so for centuries. But to my mind the mother of all of Istanbul's monuments, a monument that was built when the city was still very much Constantinople, the capital of the Eastern Roman Empire, is Hagia Sophia. And so, on the very first evening after I had arrived in Istanbul, just after depositing my luggage in my hotel room that overlooked the Taksim Square, I took a taxi to Hagia Sophia.

It was a clear and bright evening, and as my taxi skirted the coast of the Golden Horn and then the Bosphorus, with the ancient Roman wall of the city on my right, the view of the Bosphorus with its distant bridges connecting Europe and Asia, with the numerous ferries, ships and seagulls making their way, was one of those images that gets imprinted in the mindspace of an unsuspecting traveller. Soon I was at the paved square of Hagia Sophia Maidani that lies between two of Istanbul's greatest monuments—the Hagia Sophia and the

Sultan Ahmed Mosque or the 'Blue Mosque' as the English had called it. Under a hazy, blue evening sky, even to my novice eyes the similarities between the two monuments, with their lead-covered domes and tall slender minarets, separated by almost a millennium of history, was striking. Many Turkish families and tourists were out to enjoy the beautiful setting, among a swirl of hawkers selling local breads and ice creams or offering a shoe polish.

The Hagia Sophia had been built almost a millennium before it had been converted into a mosque under the rule of the new Ottoman conquerors of the city, but throughout that earlier millennium it had remained the largest cathedral in the world. Today, there are hardly any Christians left in the city, but as one enters through the portals of Hagia Sophia, Istanbul's Christian history, when it was the centre of the Eastern Church, becomes clear, as one comes face-to-face with ancient frescoes and murals depicting Mary, Jesus, the angels, saints and even various Roman emperors.

The first thing that struck me as I entered Hagia Sophia was the immense sense of space and size, as if the entire universe had turned upside down and I lay suspended somewhere in space, a mere tiny mortal. I could imagine what Emperor Justinian must have felt when he, its patron, had entered the finished cathedral for the first time. The astonished emperor is supposed to have exclaimed 'Solomon, I have surpassed you'! as the mythological/historical King Solomon's temple had till then been considered to be the epitome of human architectural achievement. And today, even after 1,500 years, the sense of jaw-dropping astonishment remains the same as one enters Hagia Sophia for the first time and stands under its immense dome. To build anything remotely close to this even today would be a miracle, but to have built this centuries ago, with handmade tools, was a tribute to the genius of those twin Greek architects, now almost forgotten, who had made it possible.

As I started becoming more conscious of my surroundings, I realized how the church had been modified and the structures and pieces had been added to it, so that it could be used as a mosque during the five centuries of Ottoman rule— for instance, the Mehraab, the place where the Sultan prayed. Today Hagia Sophia is neither a church nor a mosque but a tribute to Mustafa Kemal's modern secularism. The building that had been used as a mosque for centuries previously had been converted into a museum in a country where almost all citizens were Muslims. The ancient Roman frescoes that had been covered with plaster during the Ottoman rule had been uncovered for us to gaze and admire. So in a way Hagia Sophia represents the city of Istanbul itself; and how it has moved from period to period, from the days of the Roman Empire to that of the Ottoman period to the present modern secular republic, changing and adapting itself with time but still retaining a unique characters.

I climbed up to the ancient upper-storey galleries, walking on the same stone steps on which ancient Roman emperors and later Ottoman sultans and their retainers must have once walked. Today tourists and travellers like me were walking up, gaping with astonishment at a creation of man that appeared to be almost superhuman. I went and stood at the spot where, in the days of the Byzantine Empire, the mother of the emperor had stood to see her son being crowned below, as Hagia Sophia had remained the place where the emperor's coronation ceremony used to be conducted by the church.

The exact place where the emperor used to stand is marked by a grey stone circle on the floor, perhaps for posterity to remember.

As I looked down, I could imagine the countless coronation ceremonies that would have taken place over centuries of Roman rule, the pomp and splendour of an empire being witnessed by the mute walls and the dome of Hagia Sophia. In one corner of the upper-storey galleries lay a small gravestone, marking the place where a Venetian Doge sleeps forever, and has been doing so for the last almost eight hundred years. In the stories of the many centuries of the Byzantine Empire and of the Ottoman Sultanate, one tended to forget that for a brief interlude in its history Constantinople had been sacked and been run over by the Venetians and the Genoese, and a Latin Empire had been founded, pledging its allegiance to the distant pope of Rome. Much before the Turks, with their Islam, finally had captured Constantinople in 1453 (a year permanently marked in much of Western history) and converted it into Istanbul, Christians had been fighting among themselves, mainly and ostensibly over religion, in the streets and palaces of the city. The quest for riches and glory must have driven this Doge from his distant home in St Mark's Piazza, and little must the poor man have imagined that he had never to return. But although the Doge himself had never returned, hordes of riches of Constantinople had been taken away, across the Mediterranean Sea, and I remembered the massive and iconic bronze horses that I had seen, many years ago, over St Mark's Cathedral in Venice, witch had been taken from Constantinople as part of the 'loot', never to return.

Today, the Doge and the crusaders are forgotten, the Byzantine emperors and the Ottoman sultans are long gone, only to be written about in pages of history, but Istanbul lives on and Hagia Sophia still stands. I wonder how many more different rulers and regimes are yet to come that the walls and streets of the city of Istanbul will witness. We all are but tiny specks of dust, as the emperors and sultans were, in the long and relentless march of history.

From Alexander to Ataturk

For centuries the people who had arrived at Kuşadasi, arrived on its sea coast from across the narrow blue stretch of the Aegean Sea that separates it from the islands of Greece. From the days of the ancient Greek Civilization, through the days of the Romans, Byzantines and then the Ottomans, it had acted as a port town, and traders and armies had arrived at its harbours to trade and conquer. But as in the case of many other cities across the globe, the arrival of the railways had changed its fortunes, by ignoring it in favour of neighbouring cities, and Kusadasi had slowly languished as a rural outcrop for decades. That had been until the modern tourist arrived on its coast, this time in luxury cruise liners and Kusadasi became one of the tourist hotspots that today lines the coasts and islands of southern and eastern Europe and attracts hordes of rich and white tourists, especially in the summer months.

Fortunately for me, I arrived at Kusadasi in winter and overland, travelling on the highway from Izmir through the rugged countryside of western Turkey, through wide empty spaces between distant low hills and through orchards of oranges and olives, only rarely interrupted by a solitary house with its occupant farmer-family living their lives as their ancestors had over the centuries.

Legions of armies have marched across; under every cliff and rock lie centuries of history. The land can tell us innumerable stories, stories of kings and generals, no doubt, but also stories of ordinary farmers, perhaps of the ancestors of the farmer who sold me oranges that afternoon as I stopped briefly on the highway. The old Turkish farmer wanted a photograph with his wife but forgot, or perhaps was fearful, to ask for a copy. And so the photograph will remain somewhere in my archives and in my memory, and perhaps in his too. I was reminded of occasions when I had similarly stopped to buy guavas and mangoes from farmers in another time and in another country—similarly waiting at the edge of modern civilization for generations.

A little later Kusadasi lay sprawled beneath our feet, as we finally reached it after traversing the low hills that surround it from all sides except the one where Kusadasi faces the sea. It being off season, the city was devoid of tourists. The hotels and restaurants were taking a break, preparing themselves for the next tourist season. Many of them are housed in old establishments of another era. But the sea was a lovely blue, and the sky a lovely mauve, as the sun set somewhere far away on the horizon.

I could barely make out the distant island that my guidebook told me gave Kusadasi its name. Although I couldn't detect any special congregation of pigeons on the island, it was this bird that gave the island its name. Kusadasi is topped by an old stone castle and is connected to the mainland by a narrow tongue of land. Much earlier, when the Ottomans, who gave Kusadasi its present name, had not yet conquered it and the Latin rulers still had been ruling over it, some six centuries ago, it had called Nova Scala, the 'new port' and that itself reminded me of the precious antiquity of the surrounding habitation as we drove through the main thoroughfare to our hotel. The hotel was situated right on the sea coast, and although its interiors and personnel were from another era—when the furniture had been heavier, manners had been more formal and English had rarely been spoken—it made up for it with the excellent views that it afforded.

Later in the evening, as I took a longish and leisurely stroll along the sea coast, past the smallish harbour on my right, I caught a glimpse of Kusadasi's past, or rather one of its many pasts, as I came across an old stone gateway that stood isolated at the centre of a modern shopping area, devoid of its surrounding walls that belonged to a medieval caravanserai long gone. And yet history never stops, and I could see families enjoying an evening walk, enjoying the breeze that blew in over the blue, rippled, surface of the sea, under the steady gaze of Kemal Ataturk, whose statue stands on top of the highest hill like a sentinel over the city and the sea. In many ways, not just modern Kusadasi but the entire modern Republic of Turkey had been a creation of that momentous period in Turkey's history when this man and his followers had decided to fight and get rid of the Western forces, just after the disastrous World War I. They had created the modern republic from amidst the ruins of the Ottoman Empire. That republic for all its many trials and tribulations has survived, and rather well, as I saw the apparent prosperity and freedom of its citizens around me.

For many people like me, Kusadasi was merely a place to spend a night before visiting the ancient ruins of Ephesus the next morning, and indeed the ruins of this 2000-year-old Greco-Roman city were spectacular. As Nizam, our guide, brought out the many-layered history of this ancient legendary city of the Romans, I was struck not only by the visual similarity of the ruins with that of the Imperial Fora in Rome proper but also by how extensive the ancient Roman Empire had been. In those days when riding on horse and the only had been means of overland transport—to create an empire that spread from York in northern England to Jerusalem in modern day Israel, and from North Africa to modern-day Turkey, is mind boggling, even in today's jet-setting age. I also marvelled at the years of patient and painstaking work, mainly of Austrian archaeologists, that still continues today, to uncover and excavate the story of this almost mythical ancient city that had been lost for centuries under mounds of soil and debris of history. Today, with a little bit of imagination we can see a vision of Ephesus in place of its ruins and feel as if at any moment a Roman emperor or general, in all his exotic finery, accompanied by soldiers and courtiers, will walk down the paved high street, supervise the shops that line it, take a peek at his library, with its impressive two-storey façade, and take his appointed seat at the vast amphitheatre to watch gladiators fight. But as Nizam pointed out, Ephesus had been here, in an even more ancient version, even before the Romans or even St John the Apostle had visited it.

Today although the population of modern Turkey is almost wholly Islamic, there was a time when Christianity, under the Byzantines, and even before them under the Romans, had been the principal faith here. But even before that, in the days of Asia Minor, the ancient pantheistic religions of the ancient Greek Civilization had held sway. As living proof of those hoary days stands the Temple of Artemis, now in ruins but once one of the Seven Wonders of the World.

Even though, today, precious little remains of the once Wonder except an ancient and massive carved pillar or two, one only has to close his eyes and open his mind to imagine Alexander the Great, sitting atop his horse, Bucephalus exactly on the same spot where I stood, looking at the reconstruction of the temple, offering his help only to be refused by the proud priests who were perhaps fearful of the real intentions of the mighty conqueror.

In front of me, on top of a hill, also had stood a medieval Ottoman castle and the ruins of a Byzantine church associated with the legend of St John. In an instant the ancient Pagan Greek, Christian Byzantine and Muslim Ottoman past of Turkey revealed itself to me, even as the numerous satellite dishes dotting the city reminded me of its present.

From the days of the Temple of Artemis to the modern satellite TV, Turkey has seen all and it continues to do so and maybe 2000 years hence, some other traveller will stand over where I stood and marvel at the multi-layered history around him her, and the souls of those thousands of years and the voices of those pasts will beckon him her too.

The Mosques and Minarets of Istanbul

When I close my eyes, hordes of images of Istanbul rush in, jostling each other—the Bosphorus, shining under the silvery sun, with wide bridges spanning it, connecting Europe to Asia; ships, ferries and boats of all shapes, sizes and age sailing on its surface; the majestic dome of Hagia Sophia and the Tower of Galata. But one of the most enduring images has to be the sight of the city from north of the Golden Horn, with each of its hills being topped by majestic Ottoman mosques, with their group of grey lead domes cascading up and their tall, slender and delicate minarets with seagulls swivelling like dervishes over them.

Probably the most famous of Istanbul's mosques is the Sultan Ahmed Mosque, the zenith of Islamic art and architecture, called the 'Blue Mosque' by the English. It stands right next to Hagia Sophia, the epitome of Roman–Byzantine architecture, and the two are separated by a length of paved open courtyard called the Hagia Sophia Maidani, which many will say is the heart of Istanbul. Standing the centre of this

Maidani must be a unique experience for anyone. As I stood looking at the silhouette of the domes and the minarets of the Blue Mosque against the orange evening sky, the sound of the Azan, calling the faithful to the house of God, arose from the numerous mosques of Istanbul, as it had done over centuries past.

At first glance the Blue Mosque was not blue at all. Rather, like most of the other mosques of Ottoman Istanbul, if anything, it was grey in colour with its domes and pinnacles of minarets clad in grey lead sheets, perhaps to protect them from the corrosive winds blowing in from the nearby sea, a distinctive feature of the palaces and buildings of the Ottoman Turks. It was only when I entered the mosque, traversing the huge paved courtyard, bordered by pillared and domed arcades, that I saw that the inner walls of the royal mosque were covered with thousands and thousands of tiles, intricately ornamented in blue. These tiles, a centuries-old speciality of Turkey, are called Iznik tiles, and take their name from a place nearby, and beautiful specimens of them can be found in the galleries of Islamic art in the famous museums of the world. But nowhere else, and quite appropriately too, are the tiles quite as beautiful as in the Blue Mosque. At first glance the similarity between these tiles and the blue and white traditional Chinese porcelain seemed striking to me. And although it does appear to be far-fetched, but one has only to remember that, over thousands of years, Istanbul was actually connected with the faraway China through the Silk Route, with hundreds and thousands of camel caravans traversing miles. The world, and especially Asia and Europe, have been connected through centuries of history much more than one assumes, and nowhere is it more visible than in Istanbul, where Europe meets Asia—literally, historically and culturally.

But to me the real beauty of the tiles and decorations of the Blue Mosque lay in the fact that they never distracted the mind of the worshipper from his primary goal of prayer. The space and solemnity of the mosque could inspire a sense of peace, calm and other-worldliness in the heart of even the of most cynical of entrants. I could see peace etched on the faces of old citizens sitting on the thick carpets, with designs of red tulips weaved on them, facing the Mehraab and hence the direction of Mecca, eyes closed, communing with themselves, oblivious to the tourists milling around them.

Unlike in many Islamic countries, the mosques of Istanbul are open to the general public, even to non-Muslims, yet they remain fully functional, holy places of worship. Of course, the sultan and his grand viziers are no longer there to occupy their separate enclosures, and the dresses and manners of the people of the Republic of Turkey today are very different from those of their ancestors under the Ottoman rule, but I suspected that the thoughts and feelings running through their minds and hearts, behind their closed eyelids, would not be very different.

The Süleymaniye Mosque is both larger and older than the Blue Mosque, and in the eyes of many a visitor, both grander and more peaceful, as it is situated a bit away from the tourist heartland of Istanbul. But only the Blue Mosque has six minarets and not the usual four as in the other royal mosques of Istanbul. Incidentally, the decision of the sultan to erect six minarets on the Blue Mosque had given rise to a huge international controversy as it would have equalled the number of minarets on the Holy Mosque of Mecca, which is believed to be the most holy place in Islam. And finally the Ottoman sultan, the most powerful man in the whole Islamic world, had had to give in to the moral pressure of the religious orthodoxy and had found a compromise by helping to erect additional minarets on the Holy Mosque of Mecca!

There are so many beautiful mosques in Istanbul that after the Blue Mosque and the Süleymaniye every traveller, no matter how interested he is, has to make a decision regarding which of the other mosques he can visit. I chose the New Mosque new only in name as it is some four centuries old more because of its location than anything else. It is situated almost on the banks of the Golden Horn, very near Galata Bridge, and, besides being majestically beautiful, offers panoramic views of the city and the Bosphorus. Just as the Grand Bazaar provided revenue for the upkeep of Hagia Sophia, the Spice Bazaar provided the revenue for that of the New Mosque. Unlike the other royal mosques, which had been almost always erected by the sultans, the New Mosque is somewhat unique in that it had been inspired and been erected by a couple of queens, separated from each other by a century. Thus work on the partially built mosque had him stagnant before the second begum had completed it. Its splendour and magnificence, domes and slender minarets, spacious and calm interiors and paved courtyards still stand today, giving a tantalizing glimpse of the time when the Ottoman Empire had ruled from Turkey over a region that extended from North Africa to the Middle East and had threatened Vienna and Europe; a time when the sultan had been the holy caliph of the whole Islamic world.

When I came out the sun had too, and the courtyard of the New Mosque was full of people, both native Turks and tourists from all over the world, moving around, shopping for artefacts and souvenirs, sampling food and Turkish tea from the stalls that ringed the courtyard. For centuries this had been so, and even in those distant centuries, traders and travellers from Egypt and Maghreb, from India Persia, from Venice and Genoa from Central Asia and the Middle East would have milled around in the same courtyard, walking on the same paved stones, smoothened by scores of shuffling feet. That day, over those same stones, a Chinese girl was speaking into her iPhone; a Belgian couple was looking for the queue to enter the Mosque; a Turkish gentleman of the old order was perhaps making his way to work; an old man with a weathered face was selling Turkish coffee; and a family from distant Lucknow was looking at the amazing scenes of an amazing city unfolding in front of their eyes.

The Lanes and By-lanes of Istanbul

Since the time I could remember, Istanbul had held a mystical attraction for me, and despite the burden of huge expectations, Istanbul exceeded all expectations.

We flew in on a Turkish Airlines flight. The airline is considered among the best in Europe. Despite a long queue at immigration and an uneventful drive from Ataturk Airport to the heart of Istanbul, the first view of the old city, across the creek called Golden Horn, took my breath away. Istanbul is the only city that straddles two continents, Europe and Asia, and the strait of Bosphorus flows through the city, connecting the two continents. For centuries, from the ancient Greeks, through the long centuries of Roman Civilization when it was called Constantinople, through the centuries as the capital of the Ottoman Turks when it got its present name, to the modern Istanbul of today, the city has been unique with its unique geography, history, layered culture and people—a mix of races, languages, identities, cultures.

The European side of Istanbul is further divided into two parts by a seven-odd-kilometres-long Golden Horn that is straddled by a number of bridges along its length, out of which the most atmospheric is undoubtedly the Galata Bridge. As we walked down the European part of the city from the north, where our hotel stood near Taksim Square, through the pedestrianized street Istiklal, towards Galata Bridge, the view of the Golden Horn with numerous ferries cruising through it, of the numerous Turkish men standing on Galata Bridge with their fishing rods of the street vendors selling fish kebabs all along the coast and of the majestic domes and the slender, heaven-touching minarets of countless mosques showed us why Istanbul is called the 'city of dreams'.

Strolling along the numerous narrow lanes and by-lanes of the old city, at once exotic yet familiar to our Indian sensibilities, we walked past friendly shopkeepers selling exquisite carpets, wall-hangings, ceramic tiles, vases, lamps, jewellery and even chess boards; sometimes felt like I was in India and walking through our own Aminabad in Lucknow.

The epitome of the city is the so-called 'Grand Bazaar', a market created by imperial order of the first Ottoman emperor of Istanbul, Mehmed the Conqueror. Over the years it has grown into the largest and oldest market in the world. A walk through the narrow lanes and gates of the Grand Bazaar, with its almost 4000 well-stocked shops, twenty-two arched gates, yards and yards of arched, decorated ceilings, thousands of shopkeepers showing their wares, people belonging to all corners of the world sampling the products, is an experience in itself, even if one doesn't have the wherewithal or necessity for buying anything. To my mind the Grand Bazaar is the mother of all shopping plazas; it had been here even before Babar had dreamt of coming down to India or before Christopher Columbus had sailed to the New World.

We were persuaded into one age-old corner tea shop, where we had the most plebeian and most interesting of meals: a combination of Turkish 'chai', as tea is called in Turkish too, served in immaculately carved miniature crystal cups, along with simit—warm, crescent-shaped bread stuffed with sesame seeds. Of course, there were other delicacies on offer, from the famous Turkish delight locally called lokum, to baklavas and other sweets and savouries. But a Turkish breakfast without any pretensions or reasons to impress appeared to be simit and Turkish chai.

Despite its size, Grand Bazaar is not the only market in the city centre. The other is the famous and almost equally old Spice Bazaar or the Egyptian Market as the Turks call it. We walked through its numerous lanes and by-lanes, sampling various spices and herbs, known and unknown. I could almost visualize camel caravans unloading wares from distant exotic countries—Egypt, China, Russia, India—in the noisy and dusty lanes.

We sampled some dark, strong coffee—Turkish coffee, a favourite of mine, in one the upper storeys of an old and atmospheric restaurant, overlooking the Bosphorus and the Golden Horn. Seagulls flew over the ferries that I spotted through an old wood-framed window of the restaurant. Some bright, sunny day long ago, the father of modern Turkey and one of my childhood heroes, Mustafa Kemal, may also have looked at the scene below as he sipped 'raki'—the signature aniseed flavoured drink of Turkey that he loved so much.

Many great historical cities of the world are the sum total of their monuments, but Istanbul, undoubtedly great as its numerous monuments are, is something much more than its monuments. It is an atmosphere, a phenomenon, that has to be experienced with open eyes and an open mind.

PART 4

An Indian in India

A Short Walk through Heritage and History

It was a Sunday morning in early autumn, with clear blue skies, crisp air and a sparkle in the light. I stood at the portico of the imposing Chattar Manzil, the palace of the last nawabs of Awadh in Lucknow. Only a few months ago, a layman like me could never have ventured into these precincts as it had housed the Central Drug Research Institute (CDRI), the forbidding gates of which would have stopped curious passers-by and tourists from entering. A small white plaque proclaimed that in 1951 Prime Minister Nehru inaugurated it. I wondered what must have crossed the mind of the author of *Discovery of India* on that occasion. But perhaps the more pressing needs of nation-building and scientific reconstruction would have outweighed the importance of issues such as cultural heritage and conservation. It was unfair and difficult to judge actions of one age with the values of another.

As I entered the so-called Durbar Hall, an imposing dark hall with a high ceiling and arches that was under restoration, the image of Amjad Khan, acting as Wajid Ali Shah, meeting

Sir Richard Attenborough, acting as General Outram, in the film *Shatranj Ke Khiladi* came to mind. As I walked up the broad winding staircase, the eerie silence and emptiness of recently emptied halls and rooms greeted me. It was a scene of desolation. Signboards of different departments of the CDRI still hung on the doors and an old government calendar fluttered in the breeze that blew in from River Gomti.

Where the begums once sat in their zenana, isolated and protected from the outside world, sat later some scientist who had his entire life to create some life-saving drug. From the terrace just below the gilded umbrella, I got magnificent views of the river and the Lucknow that sprawled beyond it. I tried to imagine what Wajid Ali Shah would have seen standing on that spot more than 150 years ago. Maybe his fish-shaped bajra would have floated on the river below him. I tried to imagine what must have crossed his mind—worries about English interference, palace intrigues, his next play, a kathak presentation, a new couplet perhaps—who could say.

Next to Chattar Manzil stands another outstanding building of the same era, Kothi Farhat Baksh. The recently erected, red, sandstone plaque proclaimed that it had been built by that famous and complex French adventurer Claude Martin and later used by the nawabs for longing as its cool cavernous basement rooms had provided relief from the heat of Lucknow summers.

General Kothi next door was the house of the commander-in-chief in the nawabs' times, and used to be the offices of the senior superintendent of police (SSP) Lucknow till a few years ago and is now being restored by the Archaeological Survey of India (ASI). In fact, all these palaces and kothis had been vacated by various government departments, and so had been for Darshan Vilas Palace (which had housed offices of the State Medical Department) and Kothi Gulistan-e-Eram (which the Public Works Department had occupied until recently).

Now these buildings provide an opportunity to not showcase only the cultural heritage of Lucknow through museums, galleries, concert halls etc., but also provide the state and the citizens a chance to show the world how much they care about their history and heritage. Getting these historical buildings vacant had been one massive step. It had taken more than six decades to accomplish, and I could indeed see conservation and restoration activities in many of the buildings that I visited. But it is a long road ahead to that dream of when these palaces and kothis, beautifully restored and well lit, all along the slowly flowing Gomti, would showcase that last brilliant phase of an oriental culture, for which Lucknow was, famous all across the globe.

Katarnia ghat: Where Rare is Common

Although Dudhwa remains the only national park in Uttar Pradesh today, many consider the adjoining Katarnia ghat Wildlife Sanctuary to be even more beautiful and richer in terms of the diversity of wildlife it has. The wide stretches of River Ghagra, with all its backwaters, has riverine wildlife that is rare.

I had been hearing about Katarnia ghat for many years but it was only a few days ago, one weekend, that I had, finally *hit* the road. Though the sanctuary, nestled the border to Nepal was situated in the district of Bahraich, I had decided to take the road from Lucknow via Lakhimpur. This road may not have been as wide and as good as the national highway from Lucknow via Sitapur, but what it lacked it more than made up for in terms of the sheer desolate beauty, as it meandered along side irrigation canals and barrages, along a lone ancient railway line that ran through deep forests and lush farmlands. On that cold, foggy Saturday morning there was hardly anyone on the road, and the landscape seemed to be frozen in time.

By noon, we had reached the forest rest house campus at Katarnia ghat, which boasted of a few relatively modern-looking Tharu huts with their artificial thatched roofs, along with a more ancient but thoroughly renovated forest dak bungalow of 1870 vintage. I wondered how it must have given shelter to pioneering foresters or an occasional talukdar, out on shikar. Today, of course, post-wildlife protection laws, shikar is out of question, and the only shooting done is by tourists, with their fancy cameras.

Apart from the Katarnia ghat rest house and Tharu huts, the sanctuary, in its buffer zone, at Motipur and Kakraha, offered other accommodation facilities that could be booked online. The next morning as we had reached the jetty on the River Ghagra nearby, I had seen some early-bird tourists from Delhi, more than eager to do some 'sighting'. Thankfully, the sun was out, and the morning promised a bright and clear winter day ahead. We headed out in our motorboat, riding on the waves of one of the wider streams of Ghagra that is called 'Gerua' locally. As the sun shone, the river started showing the wildlife in its bosom, and soon there were numerous gharials and crocodiles, out to soak up the sun on the sand bars and islands that dotted the river. Here and there, one could also sight hordes of cheetals—Indian spotted deer—and even an occasional barahsingha—Uttar Pradesh's state animal—eyeing us from behind tall grasslands that stretched on the banks.

But apart from the 'sightings', the peace and bliss, as our motorboat fell silent and floated aimlessly on one of the numerous backwaters, through unspoilt wilderness, a wide sky above and dense foliage around us, made my day. This closeness to eternal nature is what must have prompted sages of ancient India to go to the forests and meditate on God. This is what must have led a Henry Thoreau to forsake 'civilization' to live a life that he had later documented in *Walden* or Bibhutibhushan Bandyopadhyay to pen *Aranyak*. As the rays of the sun shone on the wings of a kingfisher diving into the water, or as hordes of unknown black birds filled up the skies, I spotted the shining black back of a solitary dolphin, somersaulting on the surface of the silvery river. The binoculars and expensive cameras were out in full force, and the dolphin didn't disappoint them.

Across the stretch of the wide river, one could just about detect a solitary village, with its houses made of mud walls and thatched roofs, with the distant sound of radio floating across space and smoke from the household hearths suspended in the air. This was one of the few Tharu villages, home to a little-known local tribe, still clinging to its traditional but isolated way of life, against the rapidly expanding but perhaps inevitable onslaught of the modern world.

Later we undertook a land safari, on clearly demarcated jungle routes, through the heart of dense forests of mixed vegetation, as our local guide drove us in his 'gypsy' from Rampurwa's quaint colonial forest rest house to Motipur's modern tourist complex. No, we didn't see any tiger that day, although the sanctuary was known to have many, caught as they were regularly in the carefully concealed camera traps that dott the forests. But I was not disappointed. To tell the truth, even if I had had not the good luck to see even one animal or bird, I would still have been happy with just being there, in the heart of silent wilderness, away from the jungles built by human beings, to forget the heat and dust of our everyday city lives, to be close to nature, to be close to God.

Nawabganj, Swaying Lotuses and a Cup of Hot Tea

Years ago, during a long and remarkable bus journey, a fellow traveller told me about how important it was in life to extricate ourselves occasionally from our daily lives and to 'just hit the road'. Over the years I have realized the wisdom of his words again and again, and so when my mind and soul feels trapped within the labyrinthine concrete alleyways of the city and I yearn to get away from the travails when of modern urban life, I tend to leave everything and just 'hit the road', even if it only is for a short journey of a few hours.

So a few weeks ago, when dark, pregnant clouds were enveloping the sky over Lucknow, when the moist anticipation of rain was in the air, and when the breeze was just turning into a light storm, I drove over to Nawabganj Bird Sanctuary, now named Shaheed Chandrashekhar Azad Bird Sanctuary. But the destination was just an excuse for the journey itself, as I hadn't had any chance of bird-watching on that rainy afternoon. But then I was no Salim Ali; to just feel the breeze and raindrops on my face, to look at the sprawling expanses of green and at the forty-five-acre lake covered with blooming lotuses, was good enough a reason for me to go.

By the time I reached the gates of the sanctuary after a journey of nearly an hour, on the smooth highway, past the airport and the construction site of the Lucknow metro the drizzle had turned into a slight downpour. However I didn't want to stop, and so after a cup of hot milky tea at the UP Tourism restaurant, imaginatively named 'Surkhaab', I ventured out onto the recently laid cycle tracks that circumnavigate the sprawling lake. It was all still, silent and green everywhere, with an overcast sky extending from horizon to horizon. Lotuses were gently swaying in the breeze on the largely invisible surface of the lake . There were hardly any fellow travellers on that rainy afternoon, and I was glad to enjoy the solitude that it offered.

A few villagers were braving the rain and mud to harvest *Kamalkankdis* and I could see some of them carrying head-loads of their harvest home. It was a hard life for them, and I couldn't keep myself from feeling guilty in spite of being conditioned and hardened not to after years.

It was a walk of almost four kilometres on a recently upgraded and beautifully laid walking trail. By the time I returned to the tourist bungalow, despite the protection of my umbrella, I had been delightfully drenched. The sky, never bright on that day, by then had turned dusky. It was indeed tempting to stay back for the night, to listen to 'the rhythm of the falling rain', to take a leisurely morning walk next day around the slowly awakening lake. However, as so often happens in our lives, the expectations and needs of life drove me back to, city the but while on my way back I promised I would return to nature more often, to catch hold of every short break that came my way to *hit* the road.

It has been a while since I made that promise to myself!

Remembering Endless Train Journeys to Nowhere

With the passage of time, as my financial security improved and I became busier in my work life, flying became the more convenient and more preferred mode of travel, but if I had all the time in the world and no particularly pressing purpose to take a journey, I would have liked to undertake long, winding, slow and aimless journeys on train, through the great fertile plains of northern India, or through the rough and reddish Deccan Plateau or along the coastal plains of our great country.

I can remember the archived memories of my childhood: the sound of railway carriages rattling underneath, as the electricity poles swished past our open windows; the landscape that changed every second yet remained unchanged for hours together. The train would stop at small wayside railway stations, their yellow and black name boards announcing the name of the unknown place, along with its height from sea level travellers would; get down to stretch their limbs to have a smoke, to fill their water bottles and to drink some steamy, milky tea from earthen clay cups called kulhads, served by vendors who had waited patiently for hours for the arrival of the train.

Come to think of it, every railway station is a world in itself, a small microcosm of the wider world outside. There are denizens for whom this place of two-minute halts is the destination of a lifetime, is their home and workplace rolled into one. The traveller has to be satisfied with only a tantalizing glimpse of that unknowable world, as he looks around while keeping an eye on the train that will depart. Just as the sights and sounds of the huge, crowded railway stations of the megapolises have a peculiarly attractive, maddening rush and energy, as if they are perpetually on the boil, waiting for something uncertain to happen any moment, the small, half-forgotten railway stations that dot the length and breadth of the great Indian railway have a peculiar charm associated with them, and I have often wondered at the lives of the people in those one-street towns—Deoli and Shamli, Tundla and Daltonganj—as my train halts, both scheduled and unscheduled.

Although I have immensely enjoyed many of my train journeys abroad—on the bullet train in Japan, for its sheer speed; under the English Channel, for its novelty—and through the breathtakingly beautiful landscapes of Switzerland—still Indian railways, with all its heat and dust and tardiness has a peculiar appeal and excitement that is borne out of not only the immense size and diversity of our country but also sense of a huge movement taking place, a movement that may appear to be chaotic and anarchic but nevertheless is so very different from the picturesque placidness of a European train journey.

And so my most vivid recollections of train journeys have almost always been from my childhood: a huge serpentine train, almost always a dirty red in colouring rattled along vast empty plains, under a bronze-coloured sky, a dry, hot wind blowing against my face, as I sit glued wide-eyed against the iron grills of my open window, mesmerized by the kaleidoscope of life unravelling in front of me.

Slowly Down the Ganga, From Dalmau to Kalakankar

It was that time of the year when winter knocked and yet it was still not time for the woollens to come out. For years, since the time I had read the classic Eric Newby travelogue on Ganga ('Ganges' to that generation), I had had a fascination for boat journeys down the great river, through the heart of the Indo-Gangetic Plains and through the heart of the greater Indo-Gangetic Civilization. And so, as soon as I got a whiff of an invitation to join a PAC boating expedition from Gangotri to the Bay of Bengal, I eagerly joined them. Shackled as I was to the burdens of daily life expectations, I could only join for a particular stage of the expedition—from Dalmau in Raibareli district to Kalakankar in Pratapgarh district of Uttar Pradesh

I had never before been to the small town of Dalmau but was pleasantly surprised to find a grand old weather-beaten pucca ghat on the banks of the wide river, reminding me of another time when the town must have seen more prosperous days, when the ghats must have been built by some rich raja, taluqedar or courtier. It was a kayaking expedition, and although I knew all the theoretical differences between rowing, canoeing and kayaking, I had never done any kayaking before, let alone in the mighty Ganga itself. But maybe because of the encouragement of the PAC jawans, who were apparently thrilled to find me, a 'sahab', among them, I was one of the six riders on a long and narrow—too narrow for my comfort—kayak mid-stream on the Ganga.

The challenge, at least for me, was preventing the kayak, along with all six of us, from toppling over, and for some time I didn't have any chance to look at the surrounding scenery. But slowly as I started to get a hang of the thing, the pristine and time immemorial beauty of the riverine scene on both sides drew me in. Time seemed to have stopped, and the steps of an odd village bathing ghat, a temple here, a mango orchard there, some ancient fishing boats, scores of unknown birds flying overhead in ever-changing patterns and the candyfloss clouds floating in the liquid blue sky mesmerized me. I could have been kayaking in the colonial times or in the era of the great Mughals or even in the days of Ashoka or the Buddha. But I guess in those times, before the advent of railways and highways, the river would have been the original Grand Trunk Road, and the villages and towns flanking it today would have been far more important. Now like Dalmau and Kalakankar, many of them are remnants of past glory but with an unspoken, unwritten history in their bosoms.

Later in the afternoon, after an eventful journey, the highlight of which had been the inevitable topple mid-stream, we reached Kalakankar House, to a surprisingly warm reception by the local populace. I was taken to the upper, sund-renched terrace of Kalakankar House, a grand old mansion right on the banks of the river. Here the great romantic Hindi poet Sumitranandan Pant had composed his masterpieces whole being a guest of honour of the raja. As the rays of the sun reflected on millions of sparkling wavelets, I was told the remarkable tale of Stalin's daughter, Svetlana, who had arrived in this very house, as a with the ashes of her partner, Brajesh Singh, before travelling to Delhi, after a short stay Kalakankar, to seek political asylum in the United States, which she was granted. Her life, her story seemed to be the stuff of legends, and yet I had never known of her connection to Kalakankar before that sunny afternoon.

I realized how so many tales, so many stories had been lying scattered all around us. Only if we had the eyes to see and the ears to listen.

The Last Train to Nainital

Rarely does one go back to a place that one lived in once long ago, and, when one does memories and thoughts, events and persons loom out of the invisible darkness of time, across years, and something is stirred inside one as sediments of time start floating up from the depths of the mind that one forgot existed. Sometime in the last week of 2015, I undertook a journey on the Nainital Express, a train the very name of which would stir up memories and nostalgia among generations past. Over two decades ago, when I had undertaken my first journey on this quaint metre-gauge train from Charbagh Junction in Lucknow to Lalkuan in the foothills of the Himalayas, the train had already done the journey for over a century and even then had lost its pride of place to swifter trains on the broad gauge. Once upon a time, before the British left India for good the entire Secretariat and the Governor's office, along with the 'laat saab' himself, would have travelled on the same Express every summer, as the government of the then United Provinces had moved to the hills. In that way, the Nainital Express had been to the government of the United Provinces what the Kalka Mail had been to the British government of India.

Today times have changed and so has the Nainital Express. It now starts its journey from the Aishbagh Station, a not too distant but visibly poorer cousin to Charbagh and ends its journey much before the hills, at Izzatnagar, a suburb of Bareilly, famous for the Indian Veterinary Research Institute (IVRI), another British creation.

From the look of its carriages and from the never-ending rumours, Nainital Express appeared to me to be living on borrowed time, and the railway board, it seemed, might end its journey any season, perhaps forever, in this age of modernization and economic profitability. I was reminded of the branch line to St Ives in Cornwall that would have similarly been axed, only to be rescued by its good fortune for having been in the constituency of a powerful politician. Even Nainital Express happens to run between the constituencies of two powerful central ministers, but with more glamorous, swifter trains running between Lucknow and Bareilly, on the broad gauge, only an incorrigible romantic or a maverick vagabond would take the Nainital Express instead.

The first-class coupé had definitely seen far better days as the empty spaces of uprooted fittings, jammed windows and missing reading lights and missing attendants testified to in ample measure. But if I had made myself uncomfortable with these mundane things I would have missed the magnificent views of the slowly receding skyline of Lucknow as the train crossed River Gomti. The 'Monkey' Bridge and, across it the minarets of the Alamgiri Masjid, beautifully decked up for Barawafat, looked straight out of some Arabian night. The full moon overhead and its light got reflected on the shimmering surface of the river like some carelessly spread pearls and diamonds.

The train made countless stops deep in the night, at places like Sitapur, Pilibhit and Bhojipura, places that have been bypassed by the broad gauge and fortunes of time. Sometimes I think of how the railways, and now the expressways, have made and unmade the fortunes of cities and their people in a way that can be compared only to rivers doing the same for entire civilizations.

Early next morning the train finally pulled up at Izzatnagar Junction, when it was still dark, where it would rest for the day before starting its return journey to Lucknow at night. As I slowly walked away from it, past the crowd of passengers still half asleep, past the smoking kettle of a tea vendor, up and down an overbridge, to the parking lot, I wondered whether, indeed, it had been my last journey on this ancient and historical metre-gauge, 'Choti Line', and how long it would take for the ongoing march of time to envelop it back into oblivion. Reluctantly I took a vehicle for my onward journey to the Kumaon Hills. Although the newly inaugurated Bareilly–Baheri expressway was excellent, and the road journey to the foothills—through Baheri, Lalkuan, Haldwani and Kathgodam was swift and comfortable, one did miss the eager anticipation of reaching Lalkuan in Nainital Express, as in the years gone by. It was too early in the morning for the fruit vendors in Haldwani to open shop, and the wayside dhabas and colleges and towns were still in their much-deserved state of slumber. It was a public holiday, the day of Christmas (Bada-din) and nobody was in any hurry.

By the time I finally reached Nainital, the sun had been up, glittering in a clear blue sky, and the lake and the hill station were not only awake and smiling but also decked up like a bride. I was returning to the township, where I once lived long ago, after two decades. There was this strange feeling somewhere inside me—of having entered a house where I once lived but where now strangers lived. Sometime, in these intervening twenty years, Uttarakhand, a separate state, had been carved out of Uttar Pradesh, and now Nainital lived in a separate state, across an invisible yet real state boundary. Many things remained as they were, such as the Kumaon Mandal Vikas Nigam rest houses in Tallital and Sukhatal. The colourful yachts and shikaras were there in full strength on the sun drenched lake. Sardar Sons and Sher e Punjab still welcomed tourists; Hotel Grand and Manu Maharani were still there the statue of Gandhiji still stood at Tallital, and so did that of Govind Ballabh Pant at Mallital.

A few, very few, new things had come up. A statue of Dr Ambedkar, at the beginning of the Mall, now stood cheek by jowl with that of the Mahatma; the buildings of the high court had come up all around the secretariat buildings that date back to British times; and one had to wear a lifejacket while taking a ride on the boat. I remembered—it had been on this very Mall that I had taken so many leisurely walks so long ago, had stopped by roadside vendors selling roasted corn cobs or by old boatmen trying to seduce me into hiring their boat. I walked on the Mall, past the derelict library building that was perched right on the lake, past St Francis Church on my right, decorated especially for Christmas, past jovial and happy-looking tourists from the plains, past Sikh honeymooners and past hill men, with lined faces and stooped postures, as the sound of the bells of the Nanda Devi Temple floated across the lake reminding of the original guardian of the town and its people.

I am sure that when the first British settlers saw the Naini Lake for the first time, sometime in the early decades of the nineteenth century, they were reminded of their own Lake District, or if they were from Scotland, of Loch Ness. Their memories of and nostalgia for those places must have helped them to settle down and live in these parts. One can still see their remnants all around—in the Boat House Club, in the Band Stand at Mallital, in churches like the St John in the Wilderness and in names of buildings like 'The Earl's Court' or 'The Ambleside'. But one has to dig deep, really deep, through the present, enveloping one all around, through the intervening years and events recollect that to distant past.

As I left Naini Lake behind me and walked up from Mallital towards the Administrative Training Institute (ATI) and then further towards the Government Polytechnic on the Kilbury Road, I longed for a glance of recognition from some roadside tea stall owner or from some vendor of sweets in the bazaar. But of course, twenty years were just a bit too many. I walked on the flat stretch of Kilbury Road—my favourite road in Nainital—towards the Aurobindo Society Vanashram that was situated high up in the hills. All around me were delightful forests of oaks, pines and rhododendrons. A lovely breeze blew, and I could see the rays of the evening sun shining on their ever-changing leaves.

Nainital is no longer my home and will, almost certainly, never again be. I will never be able to build my hearth and livelihood in the hills of Uttarakhand, but I still think that a part of me will always wander on those hills, on those sun-drenched stretch of road, among the whispering pines and oaks.

The Lucknow I Love

Another day in my life. Another weekend in Lucknow. For the last decade or so, this city has been my home, providing me with my livelihood, hearth, comfort, succour and space. I must say that in spite of all its eccentricities, heat and dust, chaotic traffic and never-ending complaints about its crumbling heritage and inadequate modern infrastructure the city seems to have grown on me. Although I have lived in far bigger cities and have been fortunate enough to have visited many more, somehow Lucknow seems to be the only city that I can imagine as home, with its familiarity and pace of life, as easy as the River Gomti that meanders through it.

Many a summer evening have I immersed myself in the beauty of a burnished sun dipping into the Gomti, as I crossed the Nishatganj or the Monkey Bridge. Many a winter morning, as the same sun broke through a series of foggy days and smiled on the city, have I enjoyed the Lucknow delicacy of makkhan malai that some friend from the Old City lovingly brought for me. On such silvery mornings, with wispy, candy-shaped clouds lazing in the blue sky, walking along Hazratganj, observing the myriad stories unfolding all around me, has been a favourite pastime of mine. Some years ago, when my family was younger, and the number of vehicles lesser, we would hire a tonga from Banarasi Bagh and the tongawallah would take us through the heart of Hazratganj towards Rumi Gate and the great imambaras, all the time cajoling his beloved horse and behaving as if he alone owned not only the street but also the entire city. Within a kilometre we would ride past the Hanumanji Temple, the Sibtainabad Imambara and the Cathedral and would not even notice anything particularly remarkable in this.

We would marvel at the two great imambaras—the Bada or Asafi Imambara, with its magnificent Bhulbhulaiya; the Chota, with its great tajias stacked in its interior. And yet my favourite and most enduring memory would be the view of the Rumi Gate, looming in front of my eyes and then receding, as our tonga passed under the great architectural splendour of Lucknow, a virtual symbol of the city itself.

But neither does Lucknow owe its origin to the nawabs nor has it stopped evolving once the last nawab, Wajid Ali Shah, left it in 1856 for Calcutta (now Kolkata), never to return. For instance, the Indian Coffee House at Hazratganj has its own history. Here on one of its tables the great doyens of Hindi literature—Yashpal, Bhagwati Charan Verma and Amrit Lal Nagar—would congregate and talk on many an evening. Sometimes I wish that I lived in the Lucknow of those times, but still I feel fortunate enough to have heard rare old ghazals in personal baithikis at the homes of old Lucknow families, to have tasted precious recipes and to have walked under starry nights through the well-lit Hazratganj, where once Majaz Lakhnawi, the famous Urdu poet, may have walked and have penned his immortal 'Awara'.

After all, where else in this whole wide world will one get to taste desserts with names like 'Shahi Tukda' or 'Labe Mashooq'; where else can one wander into parks with names like 'Dilkusha'; and where else will one get to visit buildings with names like 'Kothi Noorbaksh' and 'Kothi Hayatbaksh'. The sounds of these names are surpassed only by their sublime meanings, and where else can one walk through that remarkable lane from Gol Darwaza to Akbari Gate—the real chowk of chowks. I can go on describing that remarkable walk, with its innumerable sights, smells, sounds and colours, but then as Kipling would say, that is another story.

The Taj Mahal, on a Full Moon Night

Although I consider myself fortunate to have visited the Taj Mahal a number of times, I had never visited the majestic monument of love on a full moon night. There is such a romantic aura associated with the beauty of the Taj on a full moon night that, although visitors are not allowed to visit the Taj Mahal after sunset, the authorities have relaxed the restriction for full moon nights, and a pre-decided, small number of visitors can visit the Taj in half hour slots. And so, on the auspicious full moon night of Holi, the biggest spring festival of north India, when the entire city of Agra was immersed in gay festivities, I found myself, with a handful of tourists, some from abroad, entering the stone- paved courtyard through the so called Eastern Gate. As the four massive red sandstone gates loomed around me in the moonlight, I realized that thousands and thousands of travellers and visitors from all over the world, over centuries of years, had walked over the same stones to visit the Taj Mahal. Soon we were walking through security to enter the Taj Mahal garden compound, and then the Taj suddenly came into view, that most anticipated and most rarely seen sight of the Taj Mahal under full moon, and yet the white marble of the Taj was not shimmering in the moonlight as I had imagined it to be. Instead the Taj stood a fair distance away—its silhouette, magnificent—under the deep night sky, floating like some ethereal dream in the air, an unreal reality. None of the visitors, for a few minutes, could take their eyes off the Taj, and the beautiful monument of an emperor's love stood mesmerizing us under the glory of the full moon on a Holi night.

And yet, to my mind the most beautiful sight of the Taj Mahal, especially on a full moon night, is from across the Yamuna, from the Archaeological Survey of Indian protected and–conserved ruins of the so-called Mehtab Bagh. As I crossed the Yamuna Bridge and drove along the shadows of the massive ramparts of the Red Fort, another UNESCO Heritage Site, magnificent in its own right, under the Musaman Burj, from where the sad, old and captive Emperor Shahjahan had used to look at his beloved queen's tomb, I was pleasantly surprised to find that all the ugly hoardings that used to line the banks of Yamuna and obstruct the view of the Taj were gone, and one could look at not only the Taj Mahal but even the distant Itmad-ud-Daula, that lesser-known gem in marble. As Mehtab means 'moon', it was likely that the Mughal emperor had got the garden laid precisely where to view the Taj on full moon nights. It is from here, across the Yamuna, with no distractions and an ideal, uncluttered distance in-between, that the entire beauty of the monument comes into perspective. It is said that in those days there were a series of beautiful gardens laid on the opposite bank of Yamuna, and one can only imagine what it feels like to take a leisurely boat ride on the river—the beautiful and fragrant gardens on one bank and the world's most beautiful marble monument on the other, with a full moon shining in a clear night sky, its glory reflected in the bosom of the river, with a gentle spring breeze in the air and stillness all around.

Today those gardens are no longer the same; the Yamuna is hardly the same navigation channel it once was; the emperors and their empire are long gone; and yet the beauty and magnificence of the Taj Mahal remains, across centuries, standing as a silent witness to the passage of the caravan of centuries.

Winters in Lucknow

This year the onset of winter got delayed a bit. Till mid-December the weather seemed to be almost like it usually during Diwali was and one could, during daytime, comfortably move around without woollens. But now one can hear the soft footsteps of the approaching winter. There is a slight chill in the breeze, and in the early mornings one can see smoky vapours coming out of the mouths of small children going to school in their winter uniform. The sun's rays have lost their vigour and warmth, and lie timidly on the land, making a quick departure early in the evenings. Dahlias and chrysanthemums are starting to bloom in the public parks and private gardens of the privileged few. One can occasionally see flocks of migratory birds gliding overhead, against the clear blue sky. In Hazratganj the ice cream and matka kulfi vendors have been replaced by vendors plying hot tea from metallic canisters. Mangoes and melons have been replaced with guavas and oranges in the fruit fare at Nishatganj.

Again, it is that time of the year when the sprawling green lawns of the Residency beckons one to spend a lazy, leisurely afternoon, doing nothing. Again, it is that time of the year when one feels like venturing into chowk, early in the morning, to savour makkhan malai—the unique Awadhi sweet that still has not been commercialized. Again, it is that time of the year, when one wants to steal a weekend to drive to the national park of Dudhwa or to the sanctuaries of Katarnia ghat and Nawabganj, or if one is more adventurous, to Chambal. As the wheat is sown, the fields outside the city wear a fresh emerald green look, and it is difficult to imagine how only a couple of weeks earlier they were vast patches of bare earth and dust.

The churches, the Cathedral, the Methodist and Christ, church, all have started their annual preparations for Christmas which is only a few days away. The gentlemen will be able to show off their ties and suits, and the genteel ladies , their silks and shawls. Many NRIs are back to their home city to escape the dark, cold winters of their adopted homelands, to find out whether their country has finally become good enough for them to return. Social circles have started to congregate at clubs and race courses during the sunny Sunday afternoons.

And yet hundreds of their unfortunate fellow men shiver through the nights, under open skies, on footpaths and railway platforms, perhaps dreaming of that day—'*Jo kabhi to ayegi*'. Who knows what goes on in their minds—a fear of the next day's travails, a helpless resignation for their present, a sense of frustration and anger at the injustice and lack of fairness of it all, a fear of some rich and spoilt drunken driver mowing them down.

The man in suit and tie at the club, the youth browsing free internet on their smartphones in newly opened cafés, families going to malls for their weekend cinema shows—all living in their own comfortable worlds, completely oblivious to those unspoken, unwashed, forgotten, almost invisible 'others'. The unbreakable barriers of class and position in our stratified society prevent one from stopping and listening to them, from looking honestly into their eyes.

It is far better to look at the smiling dahlias instead.

Waiting for the Monsoons

Last summer, being abroad, I missed the advent of the monsoons. Like most Indians, the endless waiting for the first dark clouds on the horizon, while enduring the scorching heat of the Indian plains, and then for the sound and smell of the first drops of falling rain on the hot ground has been a lifelong experience. Many a June month, in Delhi and later in Lucknow, have I rushed out to the terrace or the veranda to gaze at the rolling, dark mass of clouds that comes and covers the entire sky, at the air suddenly turning cool and moist, the fallen dry leaves flying helter-skelter, at accidentally open doors and windows flapping around noisily and the rain hitting us.

Every monsoon I remember the delightful book of Alexander Frater *Chasing the Monsoons* and the scene from David Lean's film *A Passage to India*, in which the first rain of monsoon breaks upon the courtroom just as the judgement is pronounced declaring Dr Aziz innocent. Every monsoon I remember the timeless imagery of the great Sanskrit poet

Kalidas's 'Meghdoot' as well as the tragic monsoon downpour in Ray's *Pather Panchali*. In Hindi cinema, of course, monsoon rains have been a frequent backdrop to songs, from 'Pyar hua ikrar hua' of *Shree 420* to Amitabh Bachchan and Moushumi's 'Rim jhim gire sawan' to the more recent *Wake up Sid's* song.

Every monsoon I remember my childhood days, deep inside Bastar, now in Chhattisgarh, when the hills are completely enveloped by the monsoon clouds and streams of red-coloured water red from the iron in the soil—start trickling down in cascades. When I was young and had a more romantic attitude towards life, I would imagine myself, a rucksack on my shoulders, moving from one mofussil town to another, from one cliff to another, from one farm to another, chasing the monsoon clouds over the Indian subcontinent. I would imagine myself experiencing not only the rains but also the feelings it invokes in the minds and hearts of the people of our country—the farmers, traders, students and housewives, as the thundering clouds moved in the skies, soaking everything and everyone in its wake.

I think for most Indians the monsoon is much more than a geographic and economic phenomenon; it is a melange of memories and imaginations, all rolled into one, a unique experience that most Indians miss whenever they are abroad in the months of July.

And yet again, we are nearing that last week of June, and the wait for monsoon is nearly over. One can almost feel the desperate wait of the sun-scorched souls for the monsoons to arrive any day. The last of Bada Mangals is over, and the faithful of all sects have the same hope and the same prayer on their lips. The whole country—men, women, children, animals, birds, trees, crops and even the earth—are waiting for that first heavy, pregnant rain drop. One can almost smell the peculiar fragrance that comes out from the earth, on the advent of monsoons, and hear the rhythm of the rain drops falling on the windowpanes.

Here it comes—the Indian monsoon!

Of Places and Writers, Each Creating the Other

As travel writers from far and wide congregate in Lucknow for a conclave I am reminded of how, over the years, many lands and cities have taken shape in my mind through the writings of various authors. Some of these cities I have lived in, many I have visited since, and many more I will probably never get to see, and yet the latter are not any less real to me because of the world of words created for them.

In India the one association between a place and a writer that comes foremost to my mind is that between Mussoorie and Ruskin Bond. I have lived in Mussoorie briefly in my youth and have gone back to it many a time, and yet the Landour Bazaar, Char Dukan, Lal Tibba and Kulri are forever associated in my mind with Bond's stories and memoirs. Although William Dalrymple has written extensively about distant places like the Xanadu, Palestine, Afghanistan and *our* own Hyderabad, his favourite city is probably Delhi—the *City of Djinns*, which he revisited in his *The Last Mughal*. I myself grew up in Delhi and my college was situated near Kashmiri

Gate, and while reading *The Last Mughal* many years later I could recreate entire scenes of the 1857 Uprising—rebel soldiers crossing the Yamuna to Delhi, the siege on the Ridge, the blowing up of the English Magazine and the sleepy domesticity of the Metcalfe House on the river.

Many people have written about Kolkata, internationally the most famous probably being Dominique Lapierre, but to me the writer who brought forth the life of post Partition Kolkata most vividly, with all its layered complexities has the Bengali writer Sankar, whose many books—*Chowringhee* and *The Middleman*—are thankfully now available in English. I think anybody who has read the *Chowringhee* can never walk past the Great Eastern Hotel without thinking of it.

Much before I travelled to London—Covent Garden, the Strand, the City and the Highgate were familiar terms through the numerous Dickens novels. Although many have written in and about London, the brilliance with which Charles Dickens brings out the nineteenth-century Victorian Londoner's life, with all its class barriers, darkness and details, in as say, *A Tale of Two Cities* or *Oliver Twist* is still unsurpassed. And then of course there is Baker Street with its ever-elusive 221B.

Much before I got a chance to visit Venice its magical atmosphere was brought to me by that remarkable Welsh lady Jan Morris; and who can forget the 'city of dreams' created by Orhan Pamuk for his hometown Istanbul.

There are distant lands that I have never visited but which are known to me only by the vivid images created by words. And so Chile with its long miles was introduced to me by Pablo Neruda's magical memoirs, and the rest of South America by Marquez and *The Motorcycle Diaries* of Che, but most vividly by Paul Theroux in his immortal train journey on the Patagonian Express. Similarly, I have never visited the US, but I feel as I if I have walked on the Appalachians with Bill Bryson and have floated down the Mississippi with Huckleberry Finn.

And then lastly, of my own city of Lucknow, I have thoroughly enjoyed reading Roselyn Jones, Amritlal Nagar and Yogesh Praveen, but the two books that come again and again to my mind as I wander on its heritage walks are the *Gujhista Lucknow* by Abdul Halim Sharar and *Sunlight on a Broken Column* by Attia Hosain. For years I looked for the house that Attia Hosain lived in before her migration to London, which she describes with such loving detail from memory later in her novel. And then one day, miraculously, I found it. It still stands today, guarding its secrets and memories in its bosom, right in the heart of the city. But I leave it to my readers to find those out.

Acknowledgments

First of all, my sincere thanks to my family, for their patience with me and my writing.

My sincere thanks are due to Ms Shreya Mukherjee of Rupa Publications, who took considerable pains to go through the manuscript and edited it to perfection.

But most of all, I thank the readers of my previous books who encouraged me to continue writing, in the last couple of years that it took to write the present book, now in your hands.